ILLUSTRATOR'S
REFERENCE
MANUAL
CHILDREN

ILLUSTRATOR'S
REFERENCE
MANUAL
CHILDREN

CHARTWELL
BOOKS, INC.

A QUARTO BOOK

Published by Chartwell Books
A Division of Book Sales, Inc.
110 Enterprise Avenue
Secaucus, New Jersey 07094

ISBN 1 55521 565 3

This book was designed and produced by
Quarto Publishing plc
The Old Brewery, 6 Blundell Street
London N7 9BH

Photographer: Peter Hince
Assistant: Anjuli Raychaudhuri
Stylist: Tony Williams
Designer: Karin Skånberg
Assistant art director: Chlöe Alexander
Editor: Kate Kirby
Art directors: Moira Clinch, Nick Buzzard
Editorial director: Carolyn King

Typeset by QV Typesetting, London
Manufactured in Hong Kong by Regent Publishing Services
Limited
Printed by Lee Fung Asco Printers Limited

Contents

0-18 months

18 months-3 years

3-5 years

5-10 years

10-15 years

Using the children manual

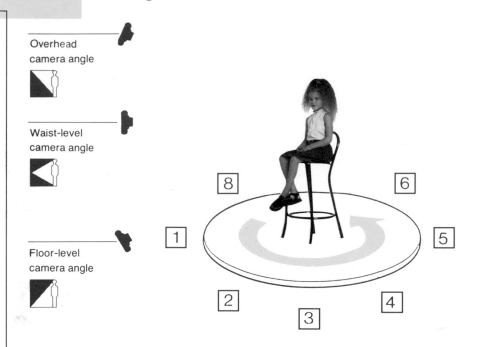

Overhead
camera angle

Waist-level
camera angle

Floor-level
camera angle

The ILLUSTRATOR'S REFERENCE MANUAL: CHILDREN comprises 112 poses categorized under five headings based on age of subject. Each category has a code number, and within each category each pose has a further subcode number for ease of reference.

Each pose is presented from 24 angles. The images are as large as the pose will conveniently allow. Consequently, although a consistent scale is maintained within the camera angles on each page, the scale changes from one page to another within the same pose. In order to facilitate the drawing of group illustrations, a simple calibrated bar accompanies each set of camera angles which are to the same scale. To draw a pose combining two or more figures, use a camera lucida to enlarge or reduce the calibrated bar on chosen angles until a precise match is obtained. This will ensure that the figures are all drawn to the same scale.

Each pose is presented from 24 angles, achieved by using three cameras, and a turntable rotated through 360° (above). A simple camera angle symbol (above left) accompanies the relevant group of images within a pose.

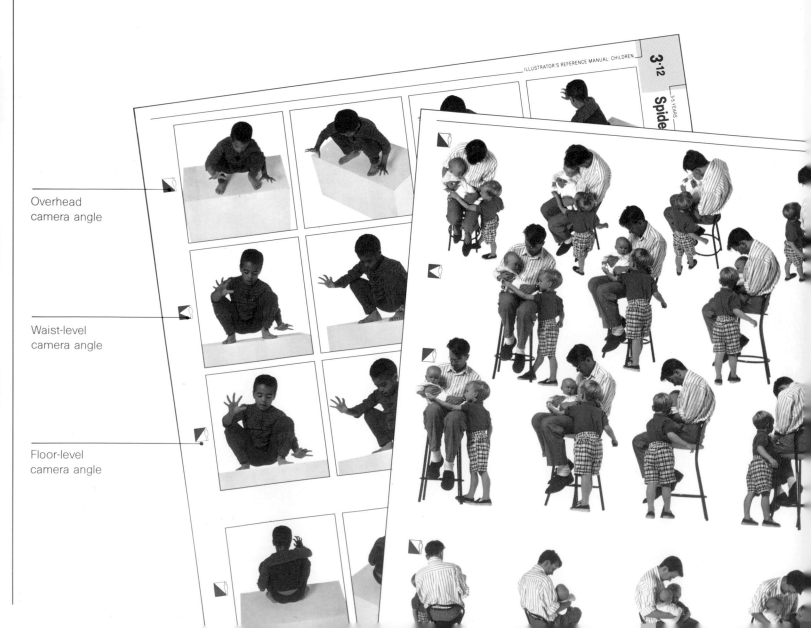

Overhead
camera angle

Waist-level
camera angle

Floor-level
camera angle

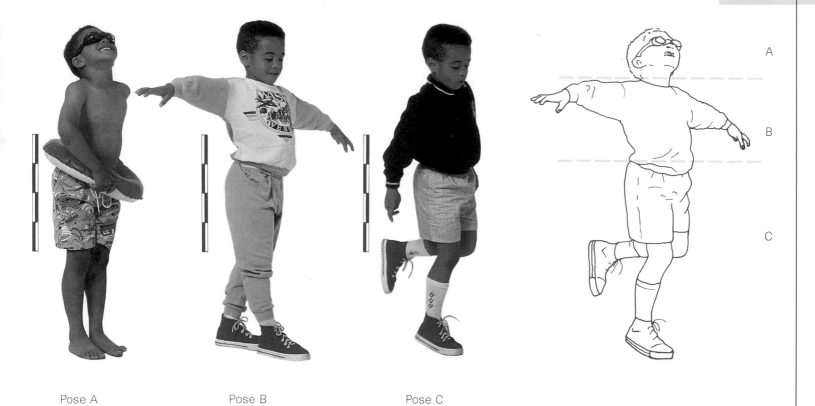

A

B

C

Pose A   Pose B   Pose C

Composite figures (above) can be drawn using elements from different poses. The calibrated bar allows elements from poses presented in different scales to be combined.

Group illustrations (below) can easily be drawn. The calibrated bar accompanying each pose can be used to standardize the scales.

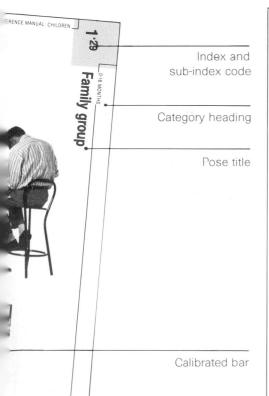

ERENCE MANUAL: CHILDREN

1·29

0–18 MONTHS

Family group

Index and sub-index code

Category heading

Pose title

Calibrated bar

1·01

Mother holding baby

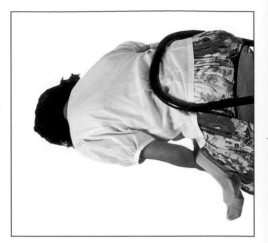

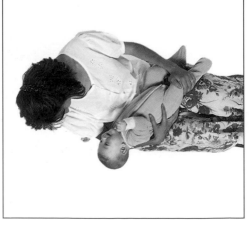

Mother holding baby

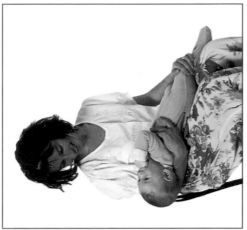

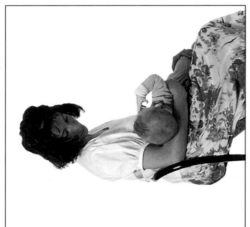
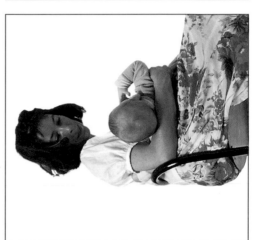

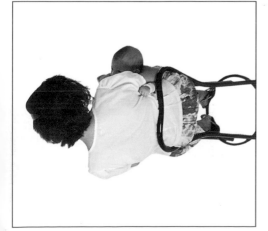

1·02 Nursing

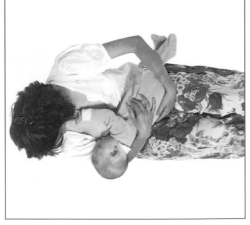

ILLUSTRATOR'S REFERENCE MANUAL: CHILDREN

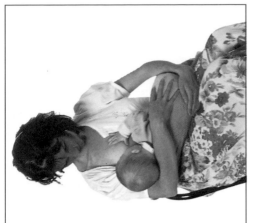

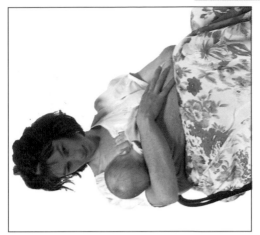

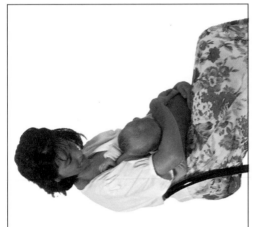

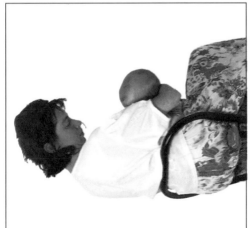

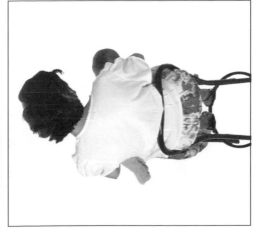

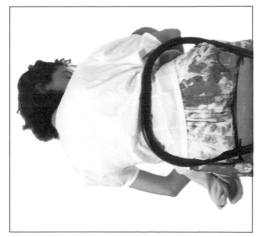

Bubbling baby

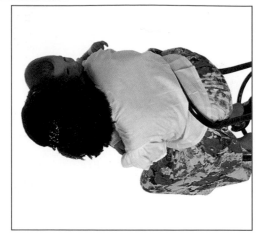

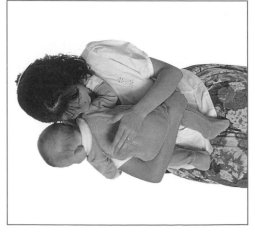

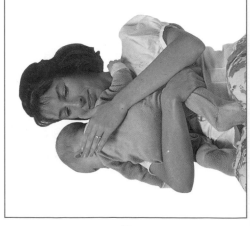

Bubbling baby

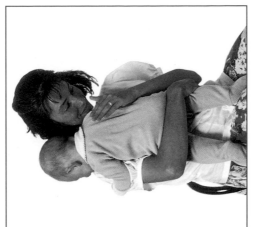

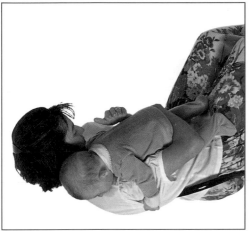
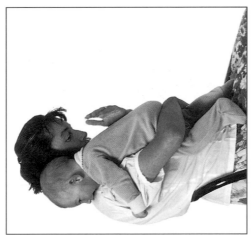

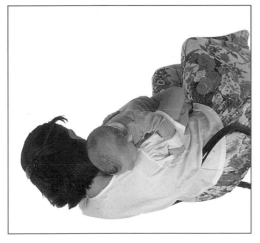
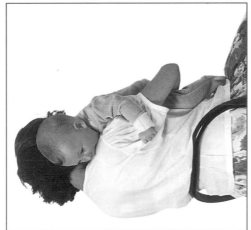
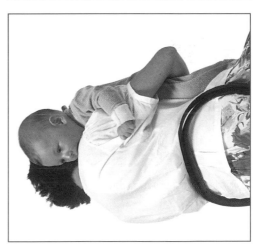

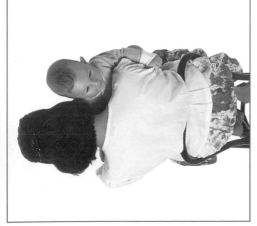

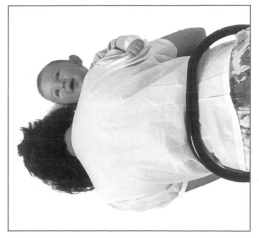

1·04 Carried in a baby sling

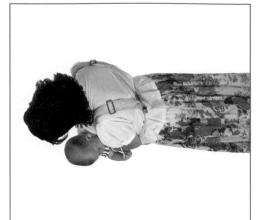

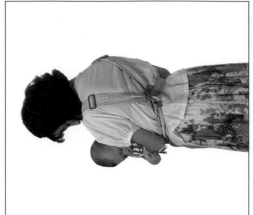

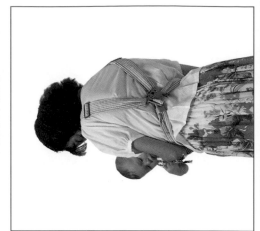

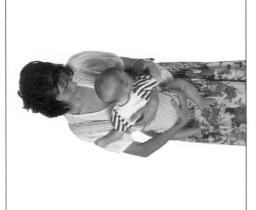

Carried in a baby sling

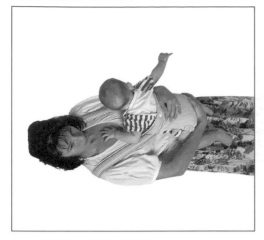

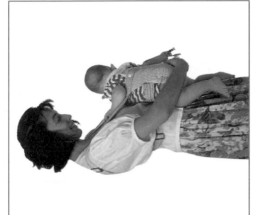

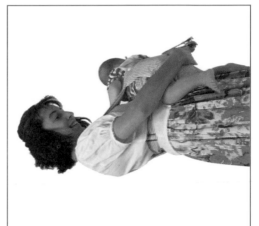

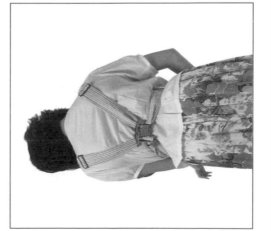

1·05 Bathtime

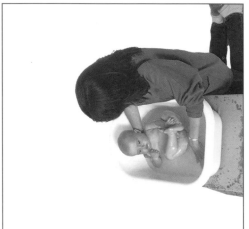

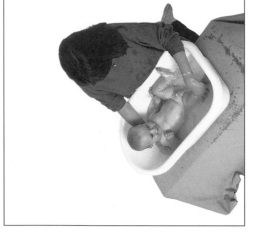

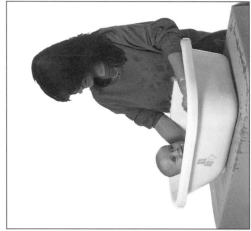

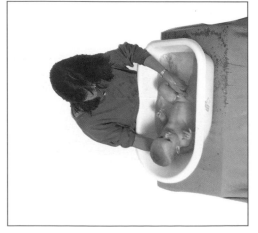

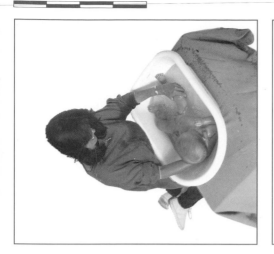

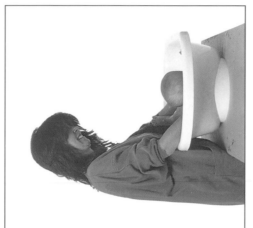

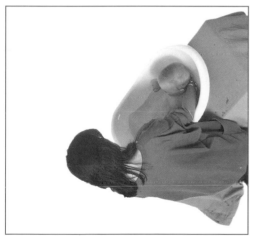
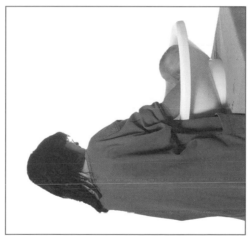

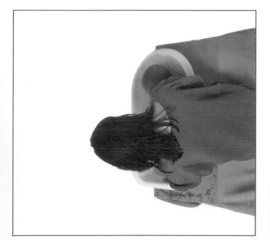
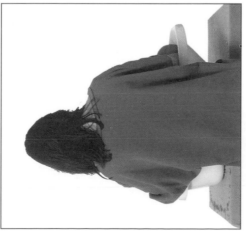

1·06

Diaper changing

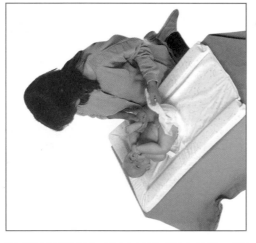

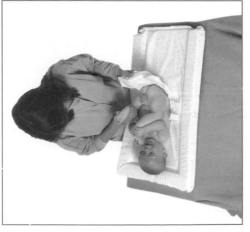
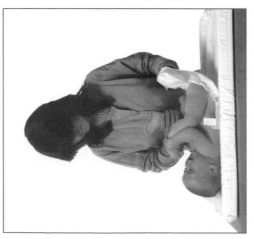

ILLUSTRATOR'S REFERENCE MANUAL: CHILDREN

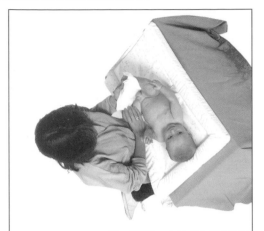

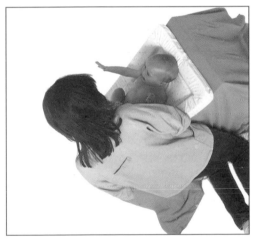

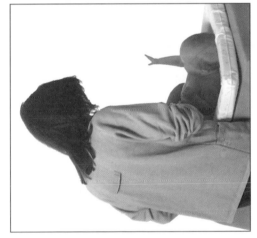

1·07

Drying baby

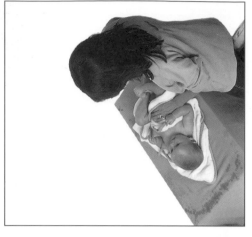

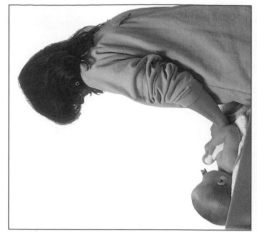

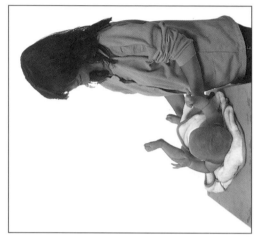

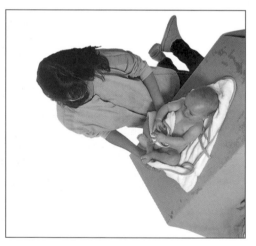

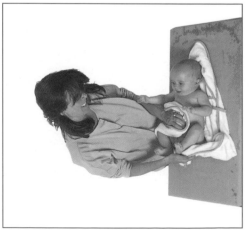

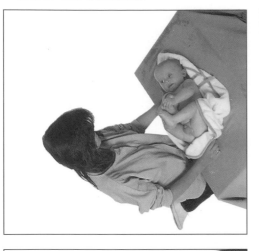
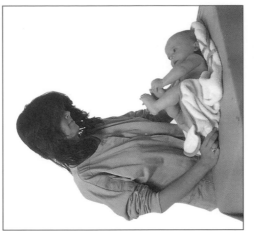

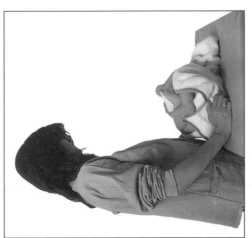
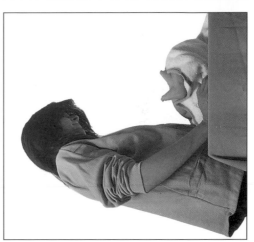

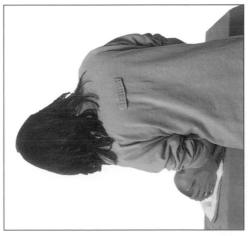

1·08 Being dressed

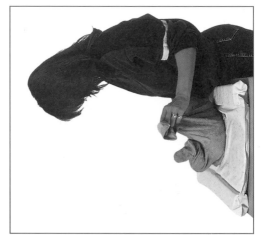

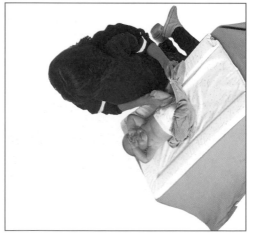

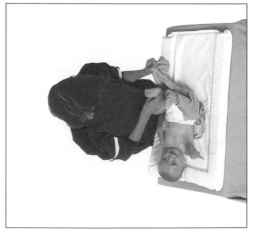

Being dressed

ILLUSTRATOR'S REFERENCE MANUAL: CHILDREN

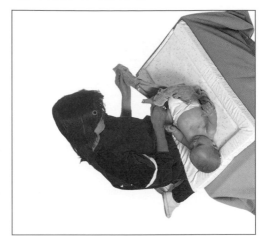

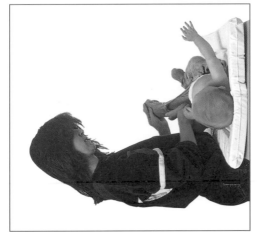
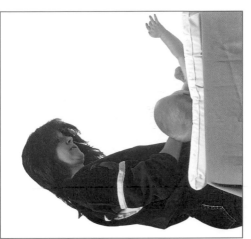

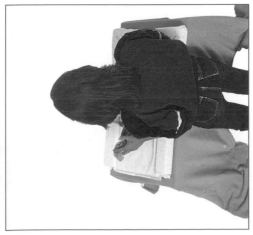

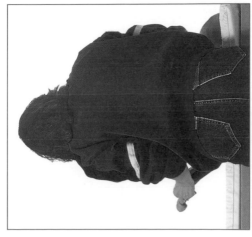

Up in the air

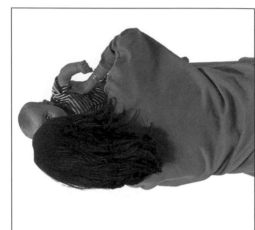

Up in the air

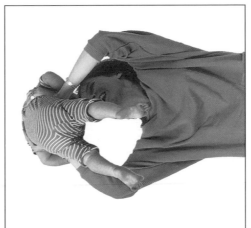

1·10

A bottlefeeding from daddy

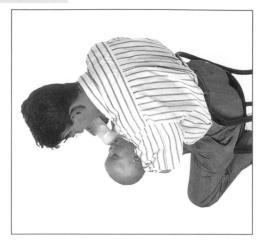

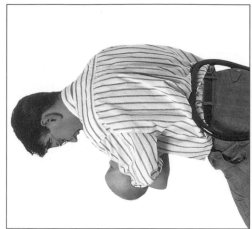

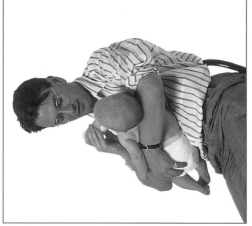

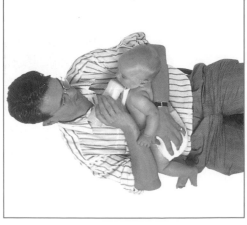

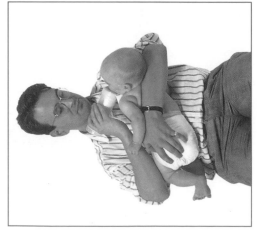

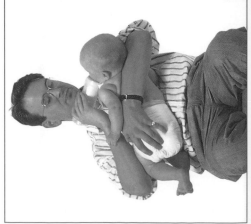

A bottlefeeding from daddy

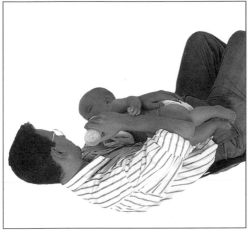

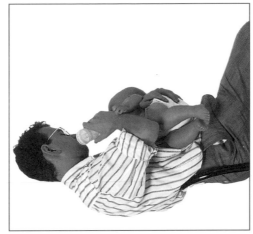

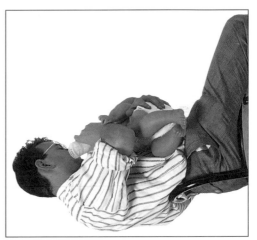

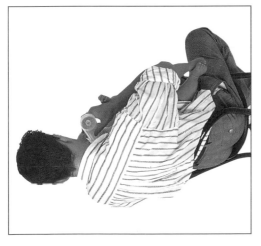

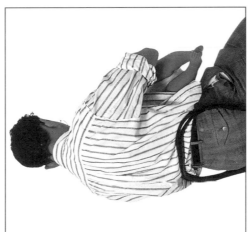

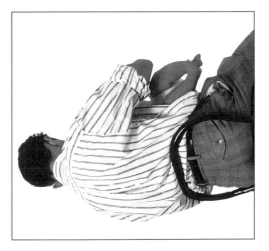

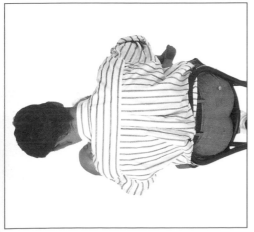

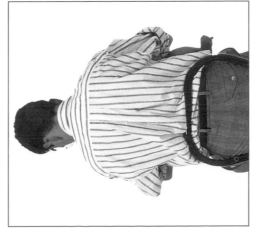

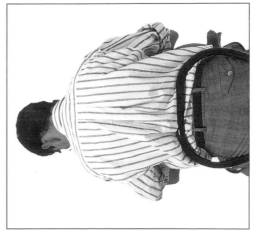

1·11 Wrapped in a shawl

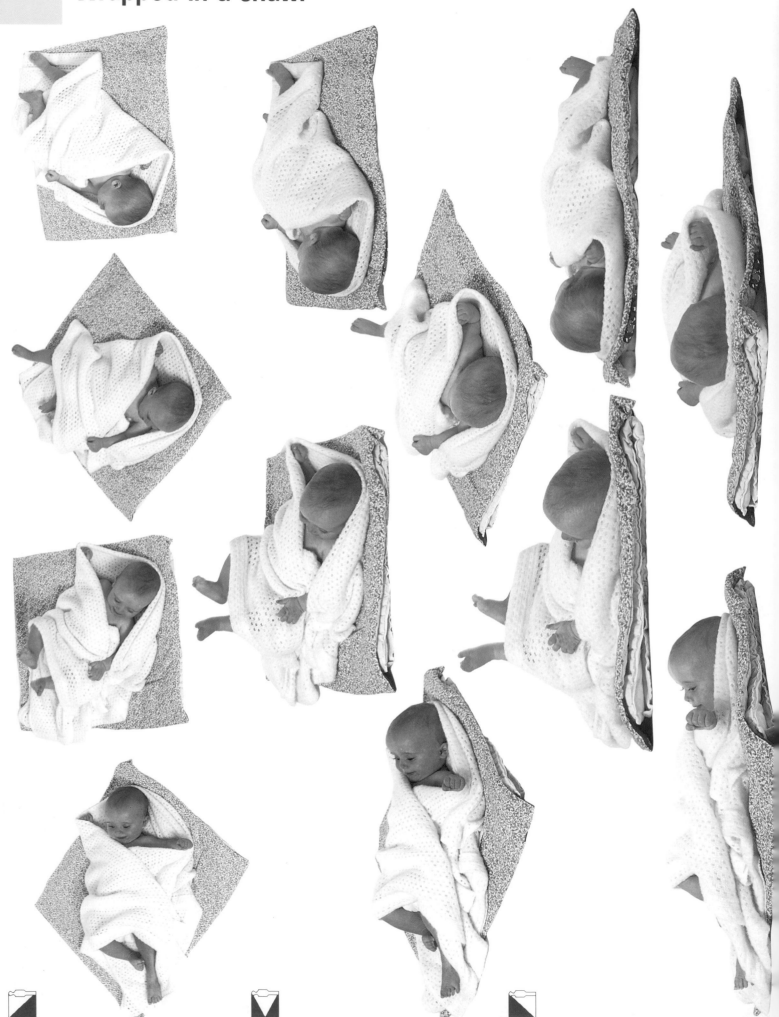

Wrapped in a shawl

1·12

Having a snooze

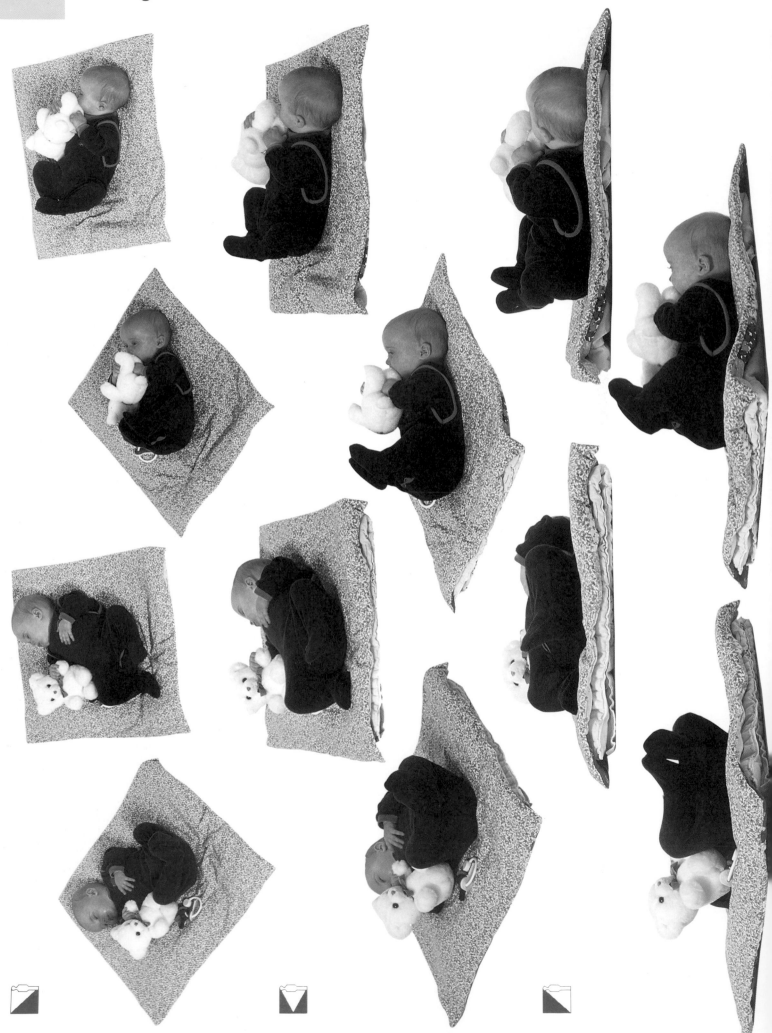

Having a snooze

Lying on back crying

Lying on back crying

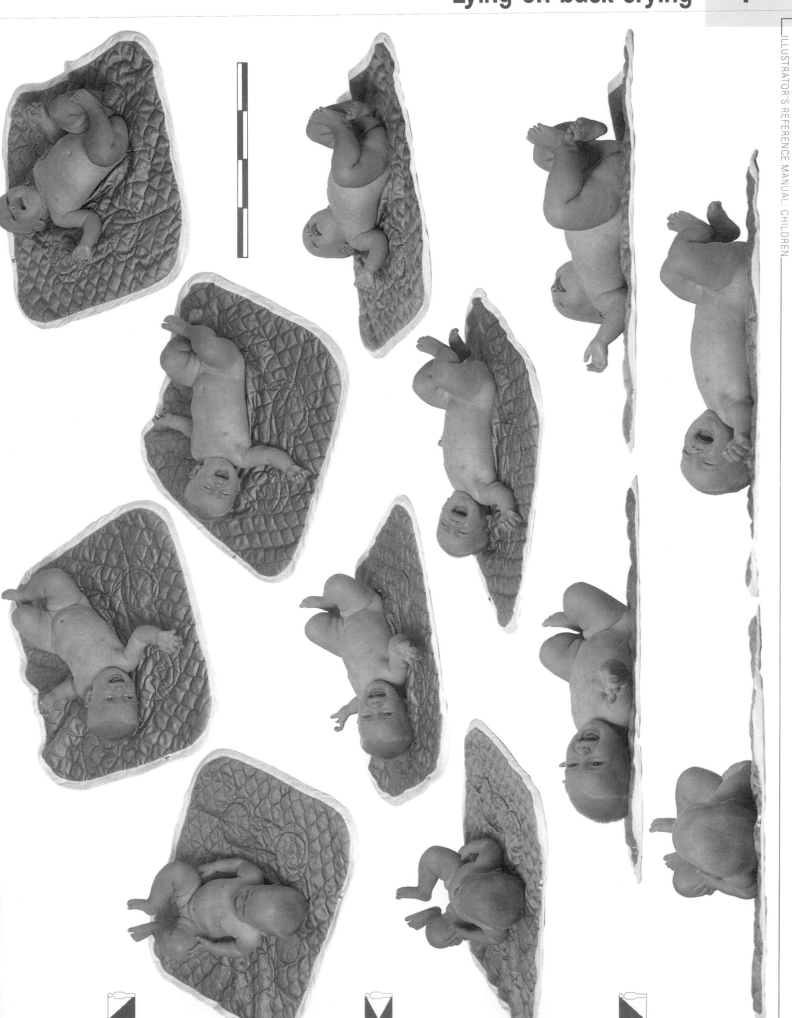

Lying on stomach laughing

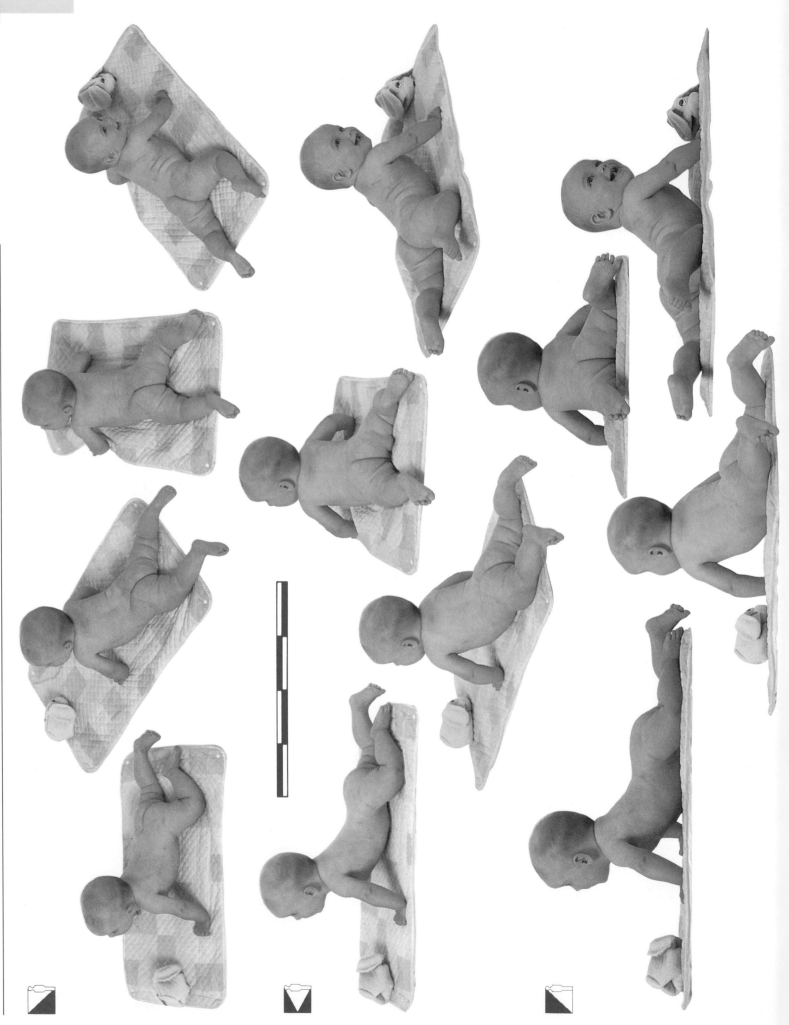

Lying on stomach laughing

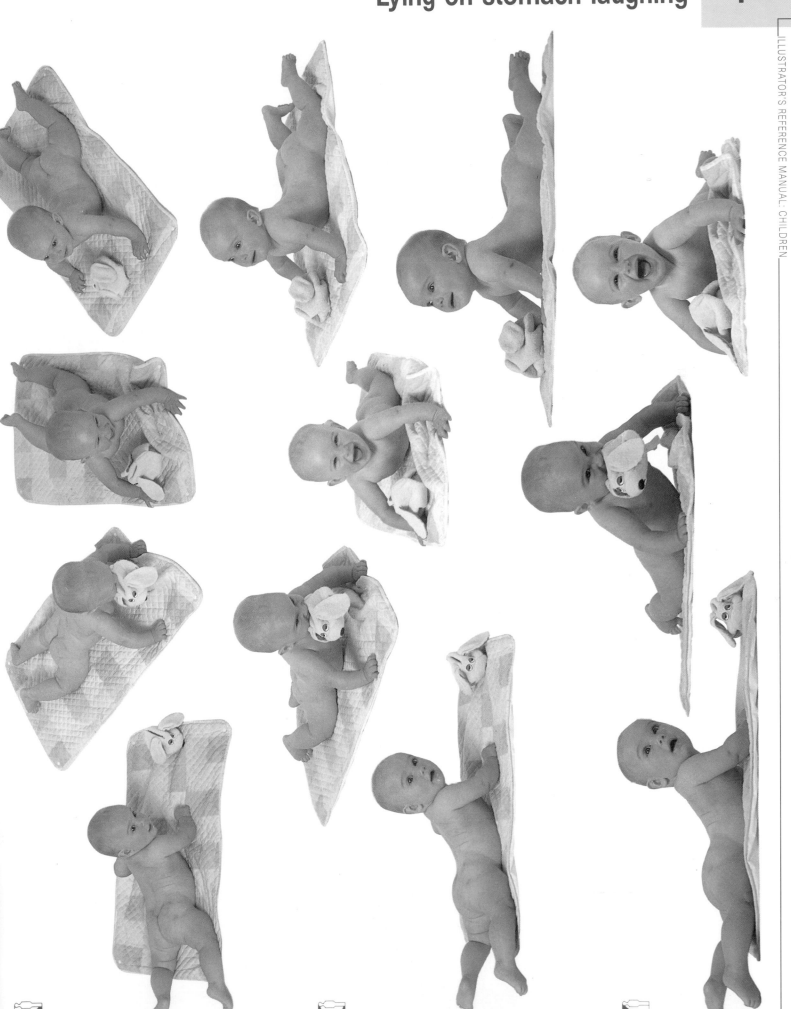

1·15

Lying in carriage

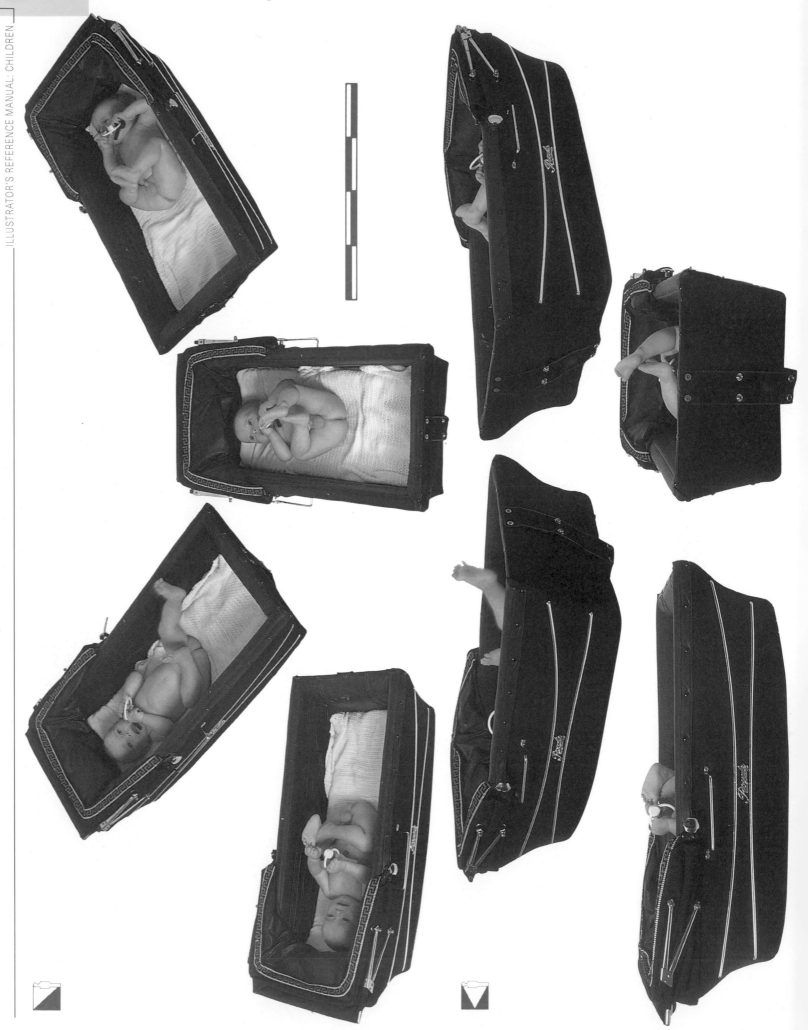

Lying in carriage

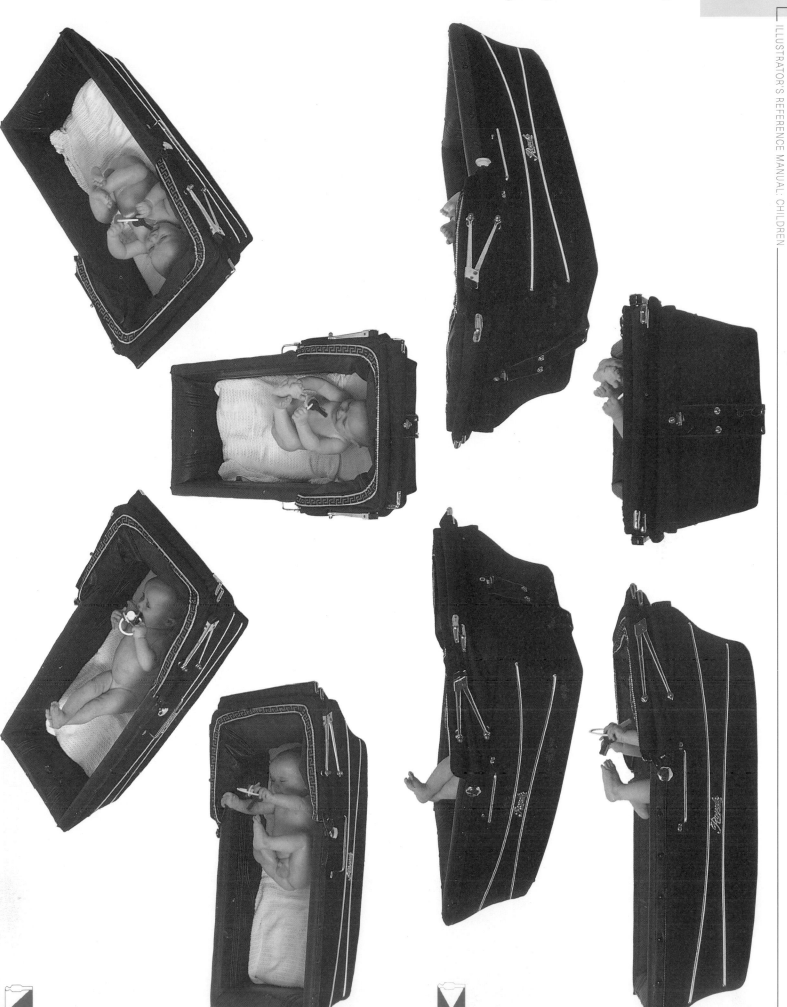

1·16

On the potty

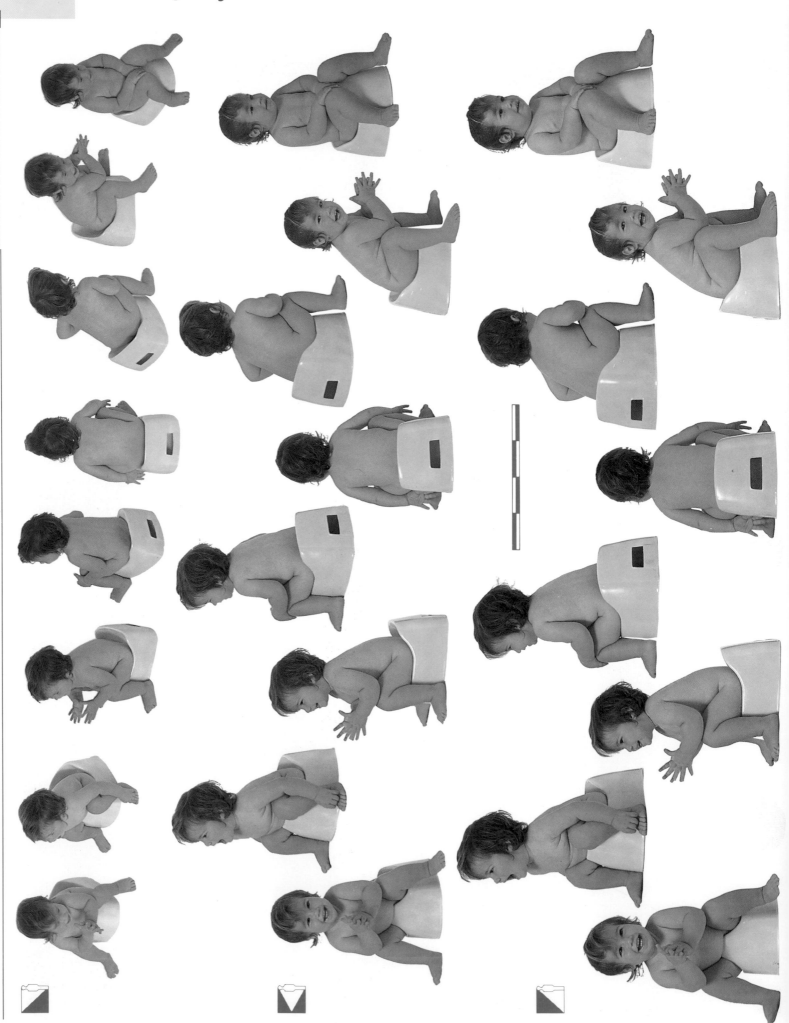

Sitting in diaper

1·18

Taking teddy for a trip

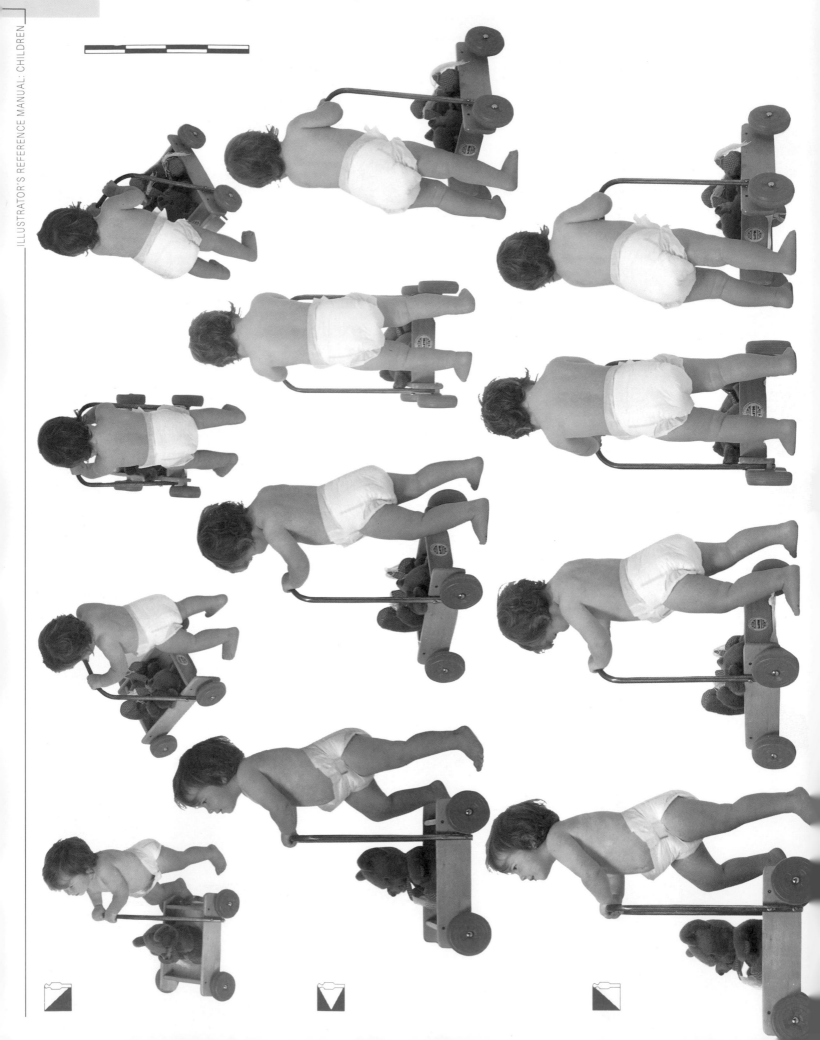

Taking teddy for a trip

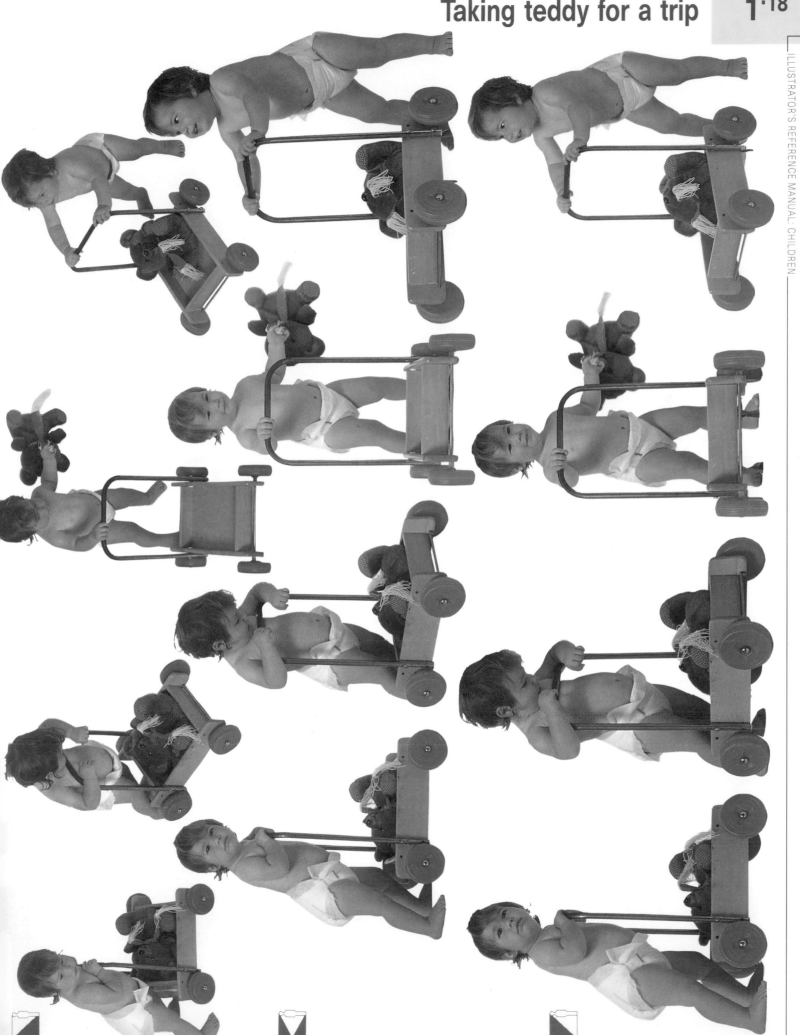

1·19

First steps

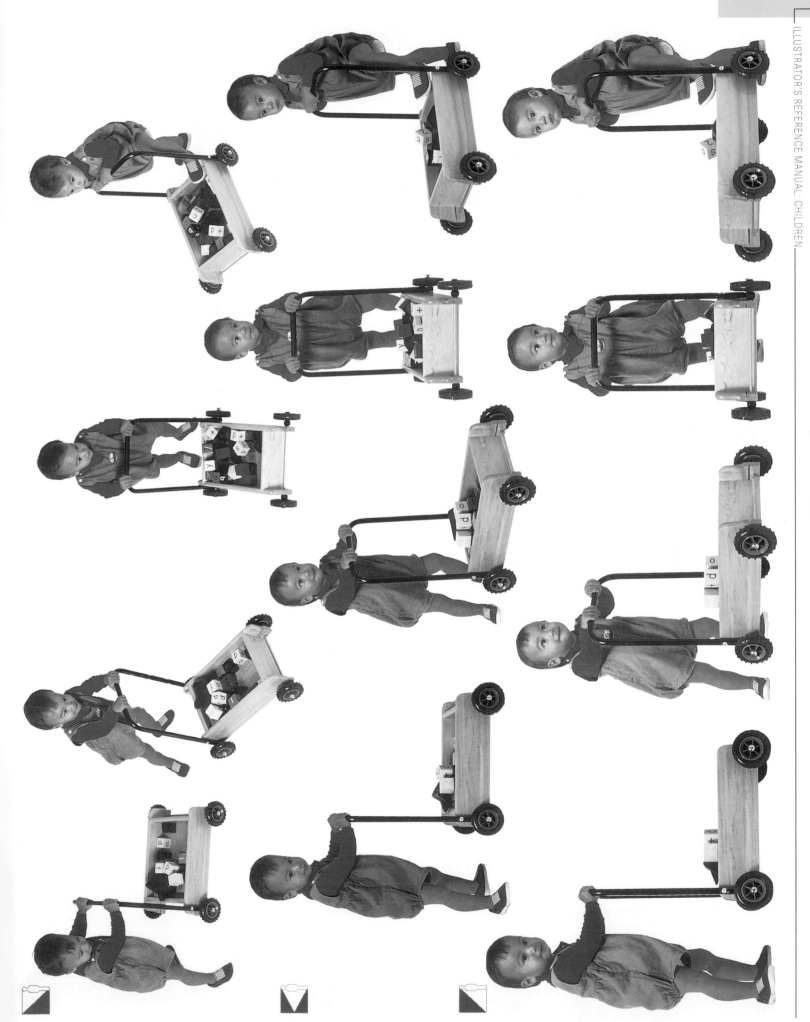

1·20 Playing the tambourine

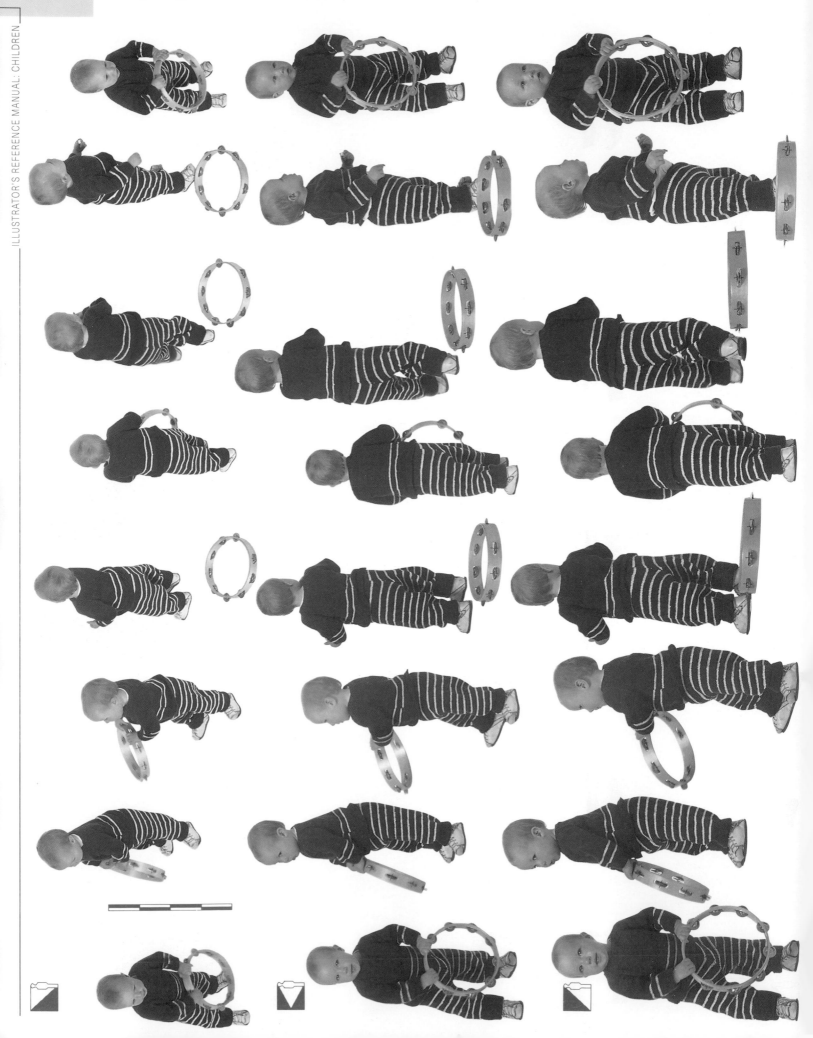

Standing in winter clothes

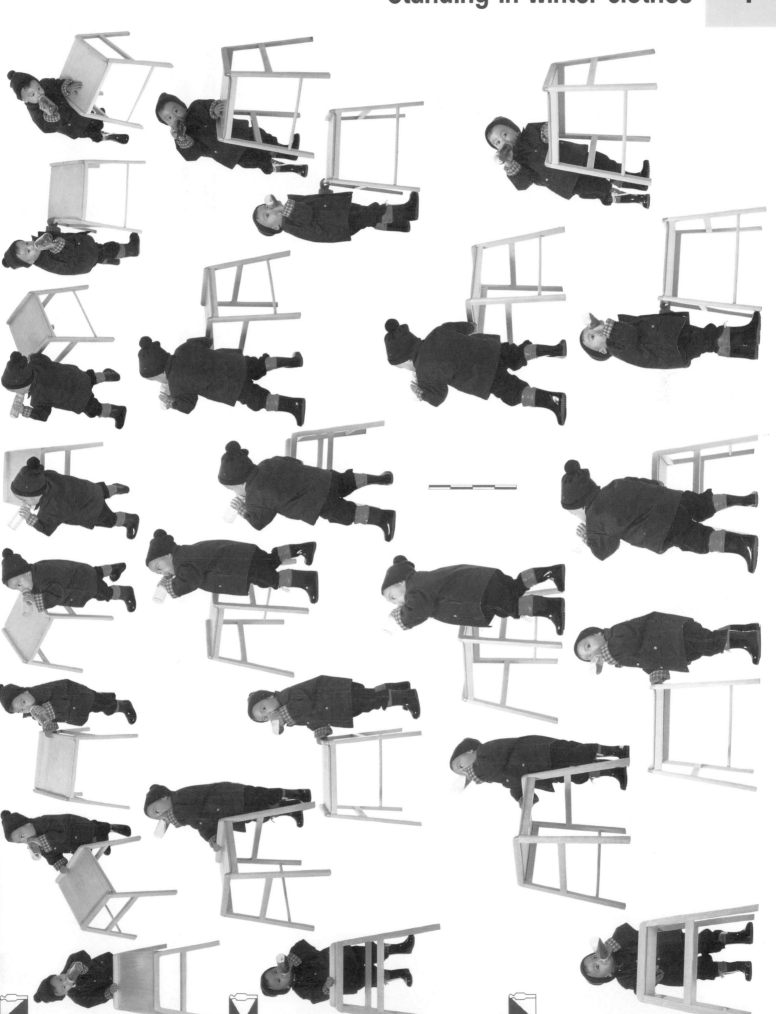

1·22 Playing with toy plane

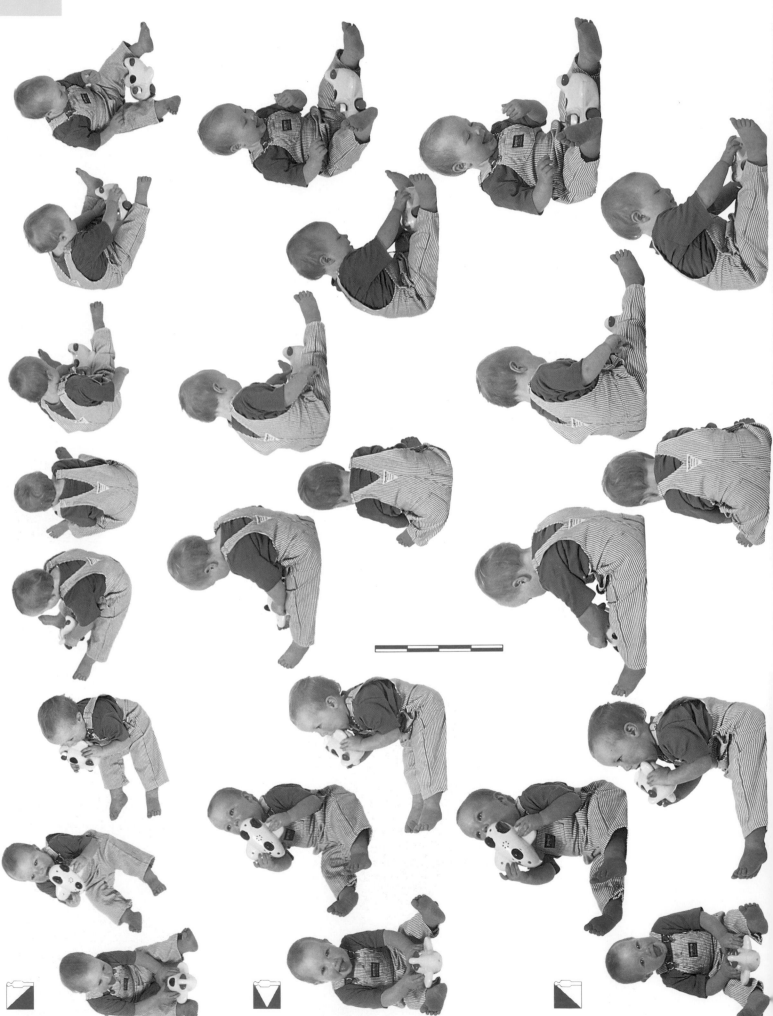

Figuring it out

1·24

A game before bedtime

A game before bedtime

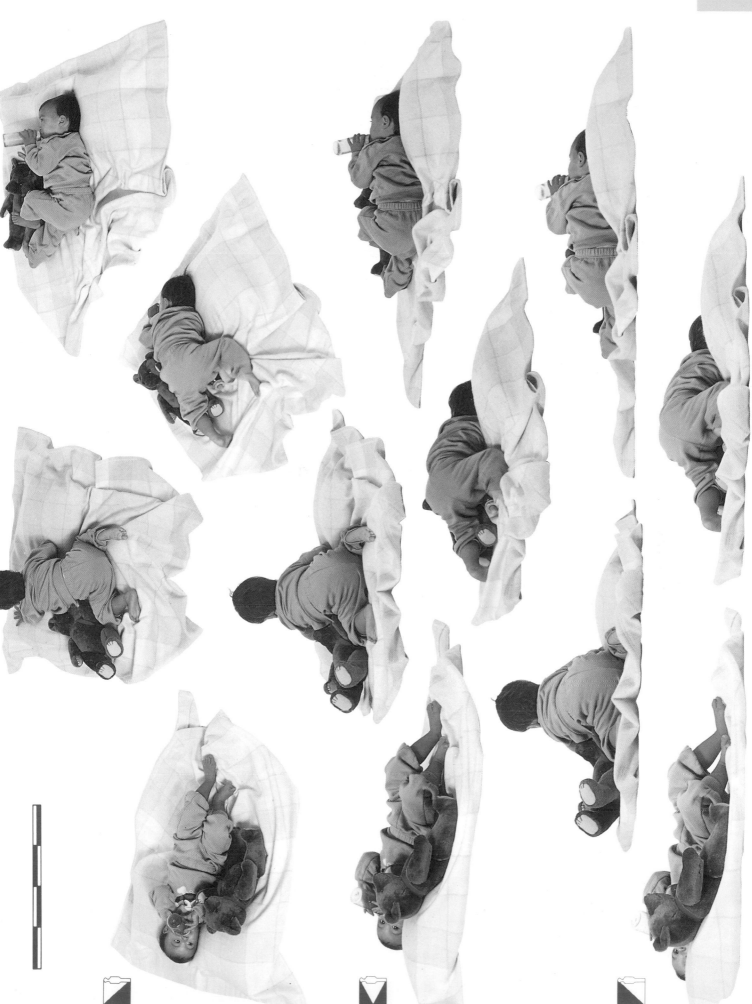

1·25

Riding a rocking horse

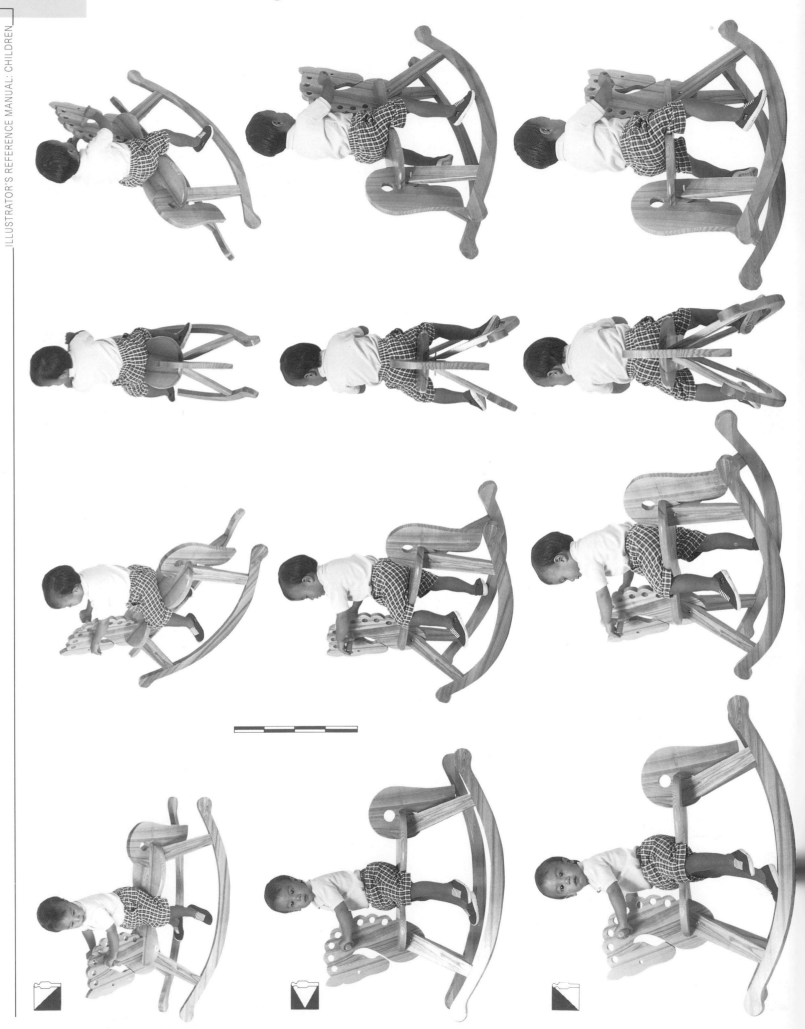

Riding a rocking horse

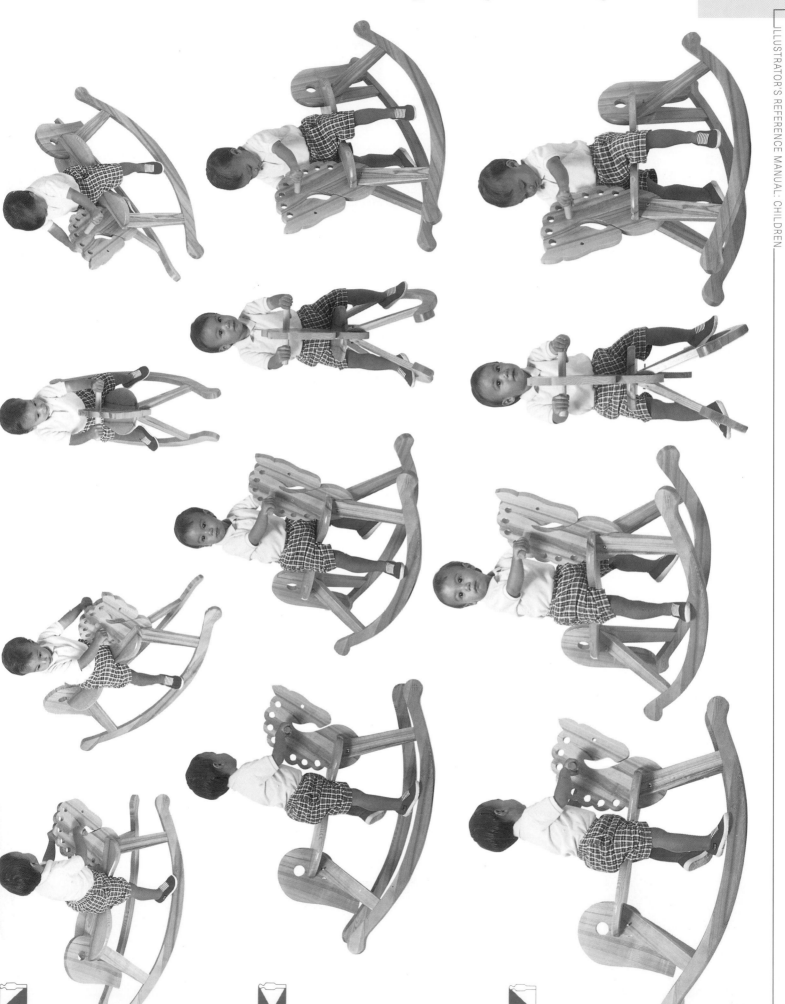

Sitting in highchair

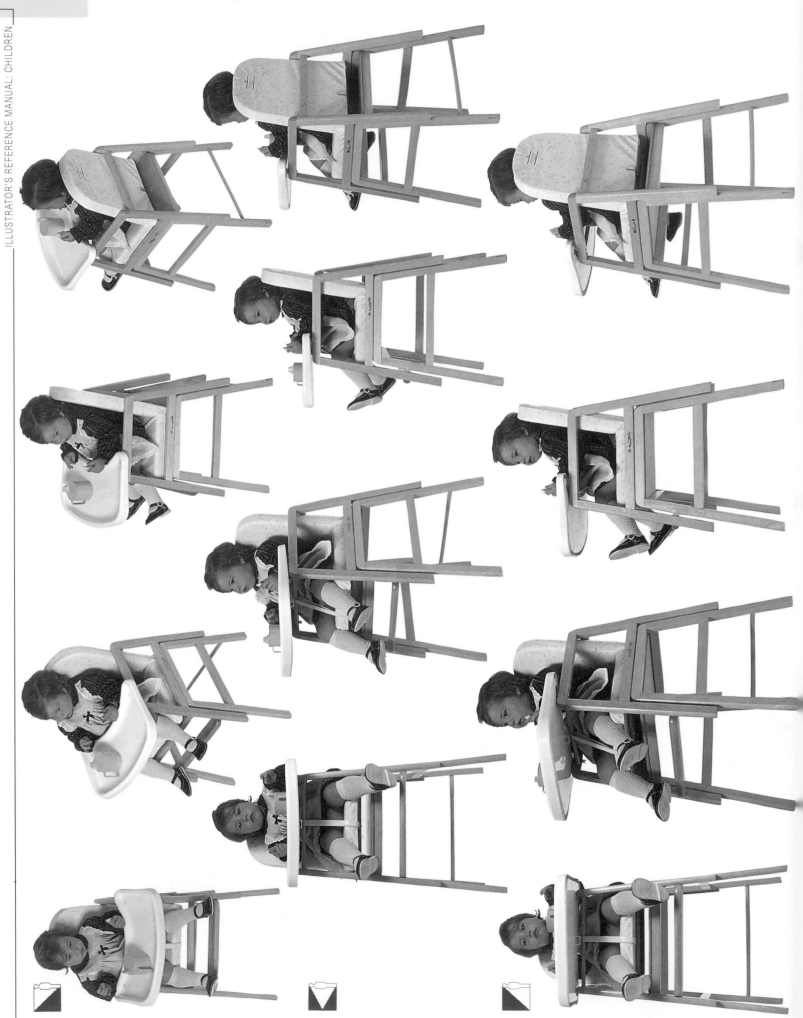

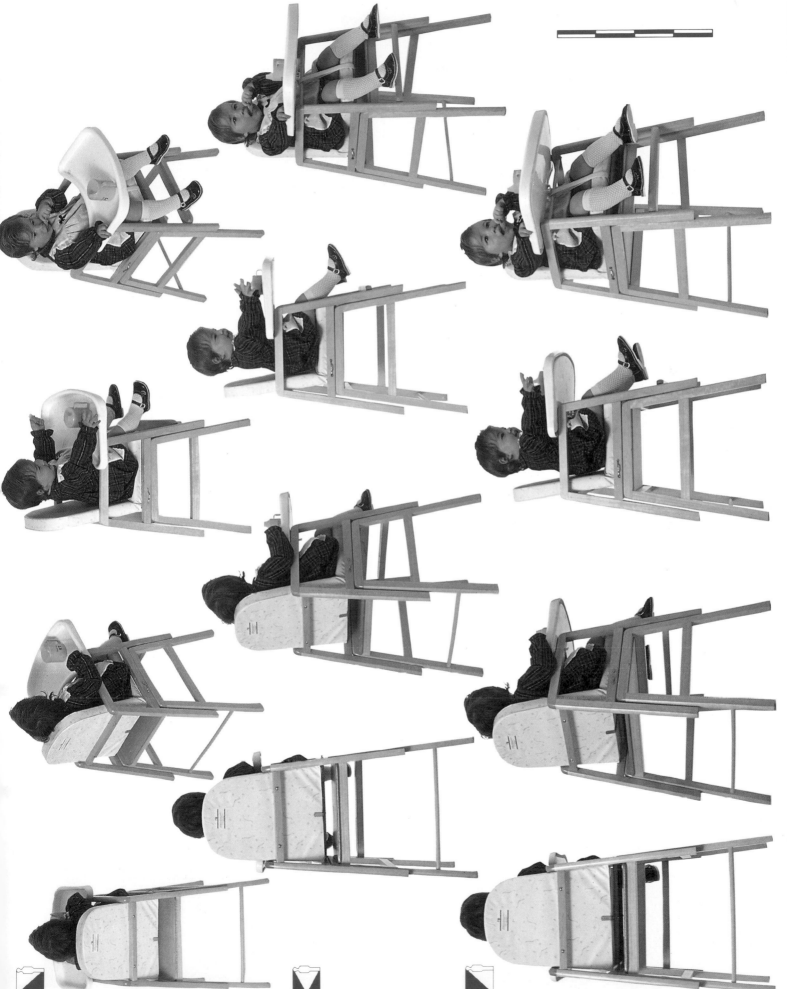

1·27

A ride in a stroller

A ride in a stroller

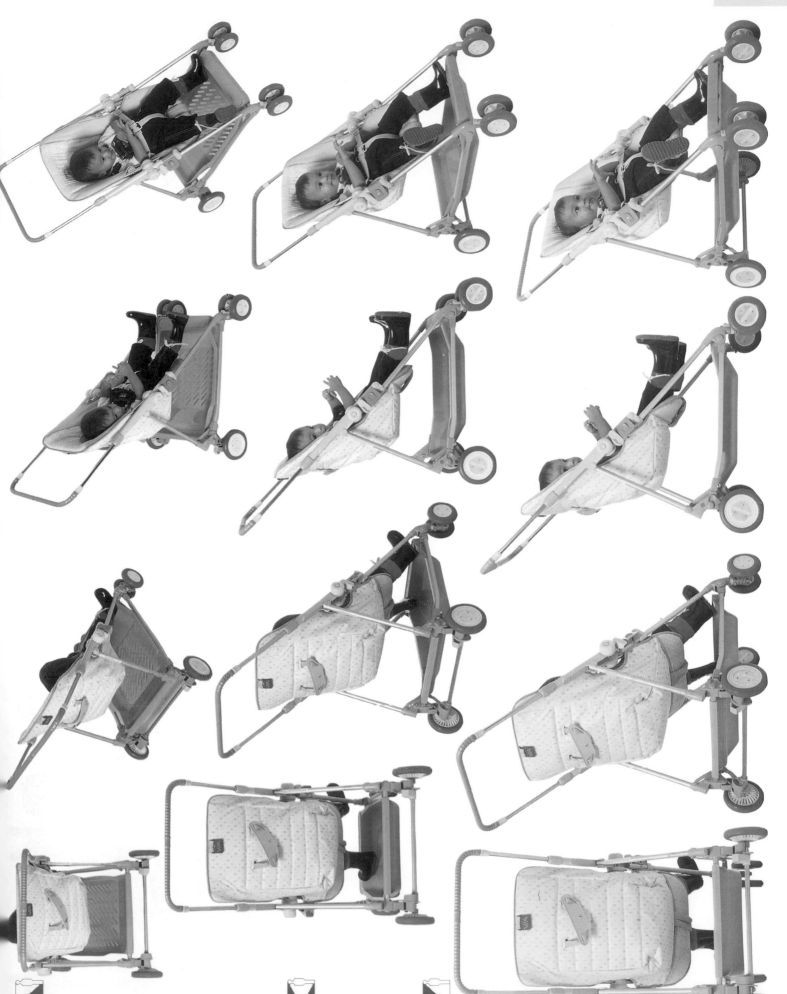

1·28 Comforting baby sister

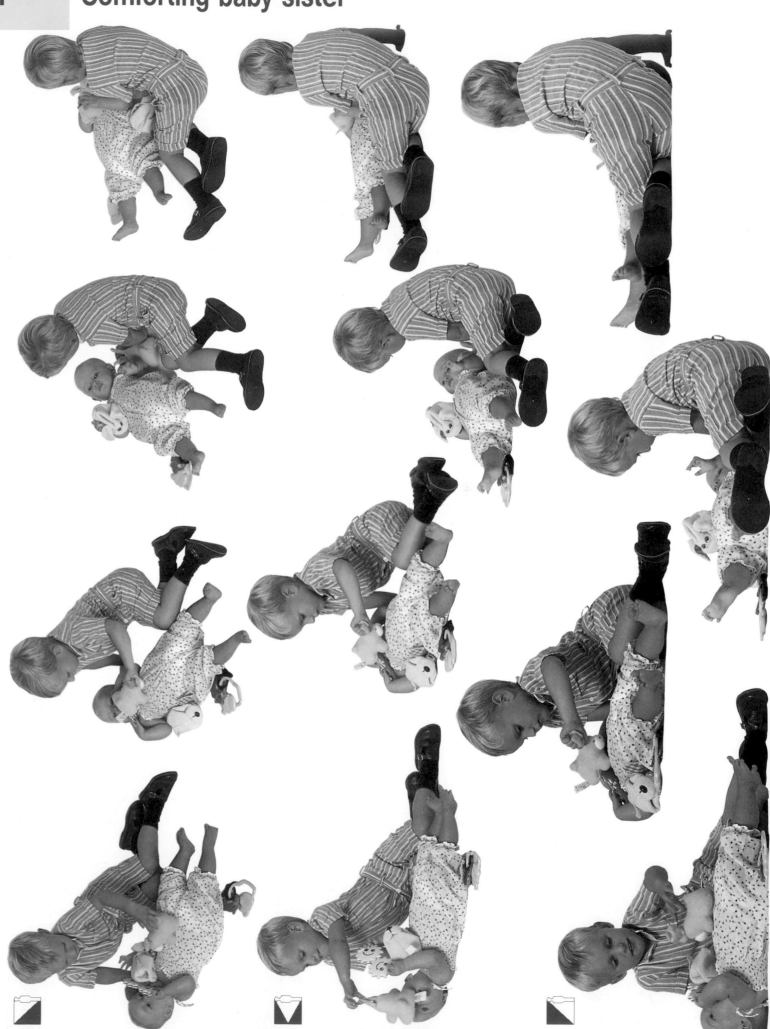

Comforting baby sister

1·29 Family group

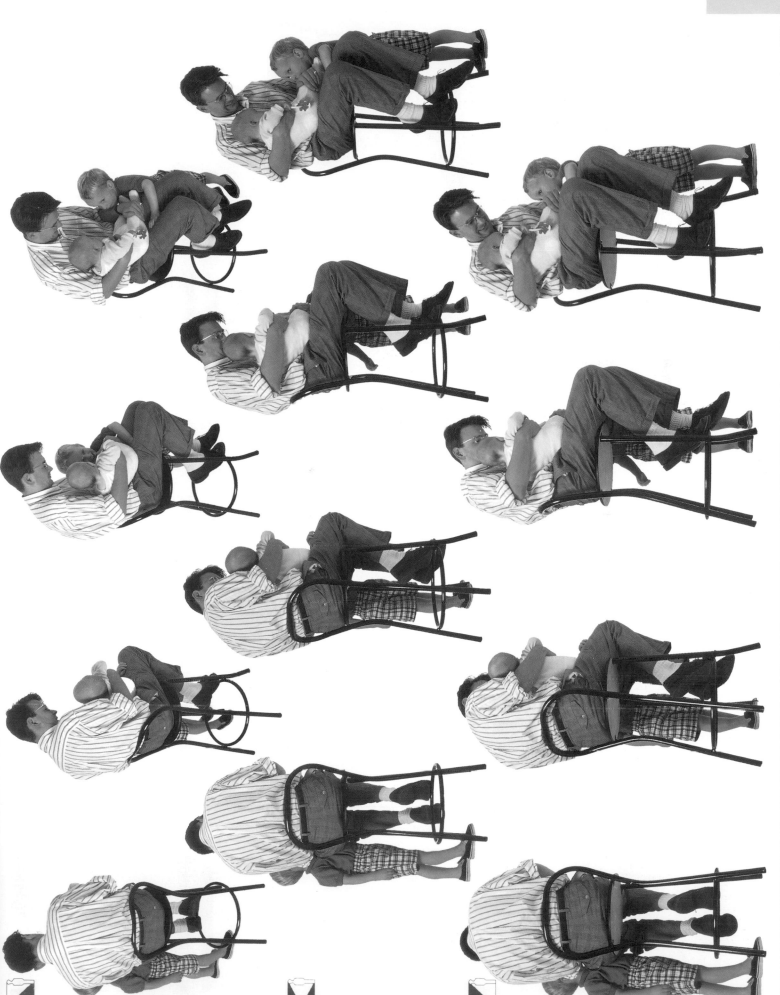

2·01 **Enjoying a treat**

Looking at picture books

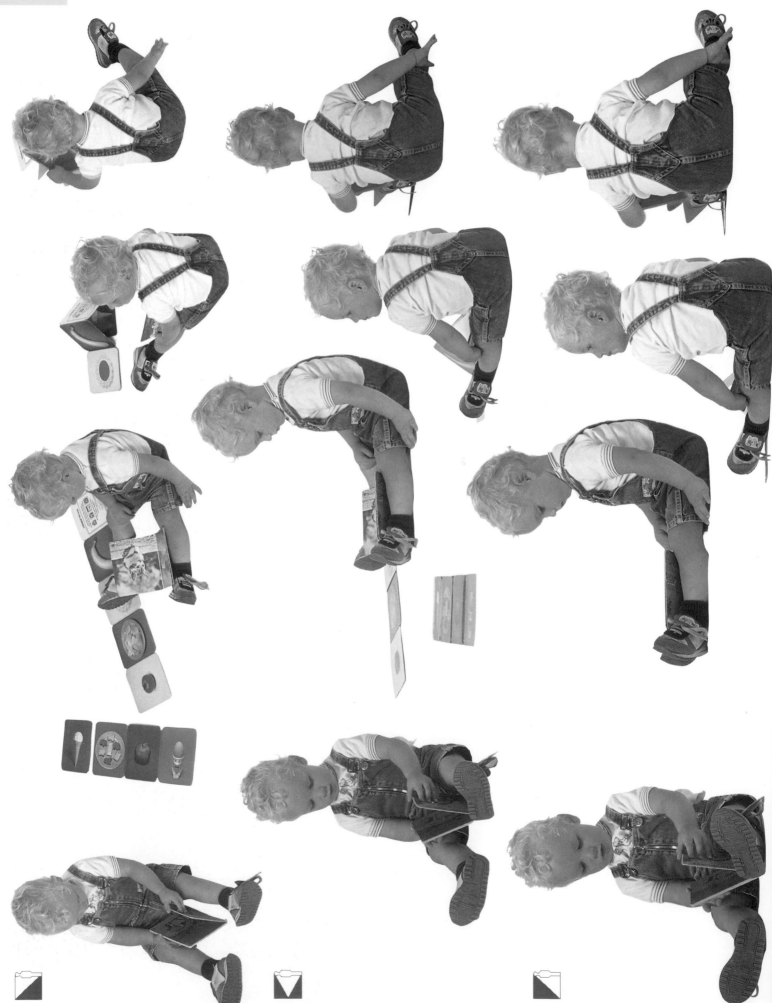

Looking at picture books

2·04 # Teddy bear's picnic

2·05

What's in the toybox?

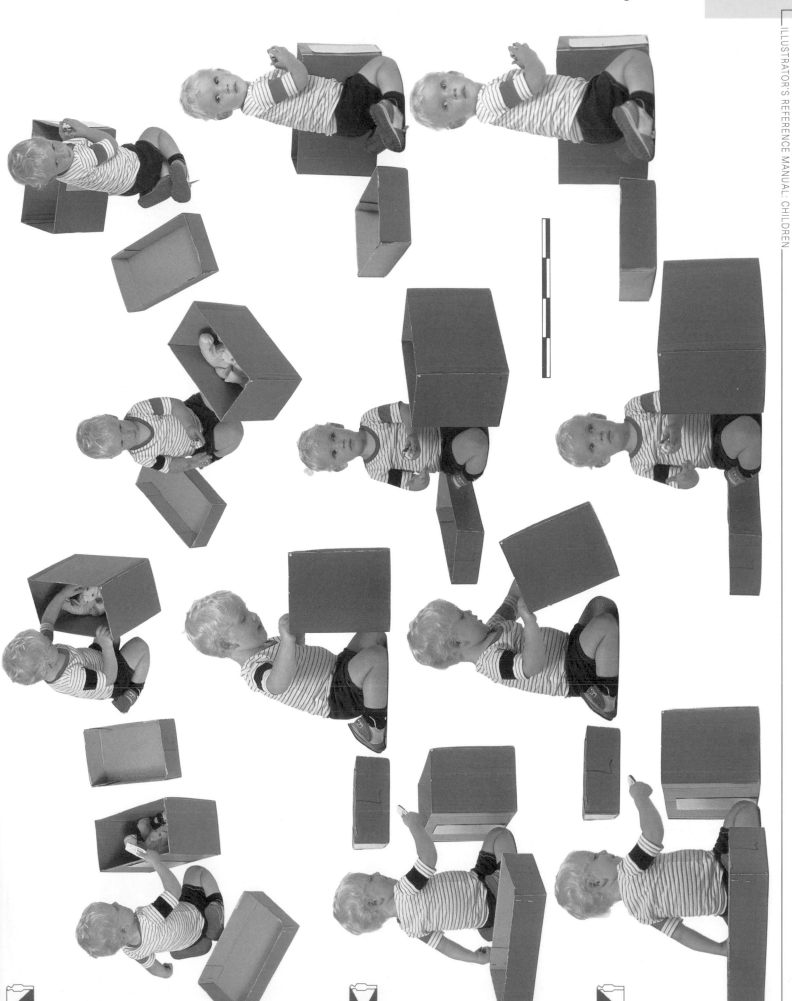

A box of surprises

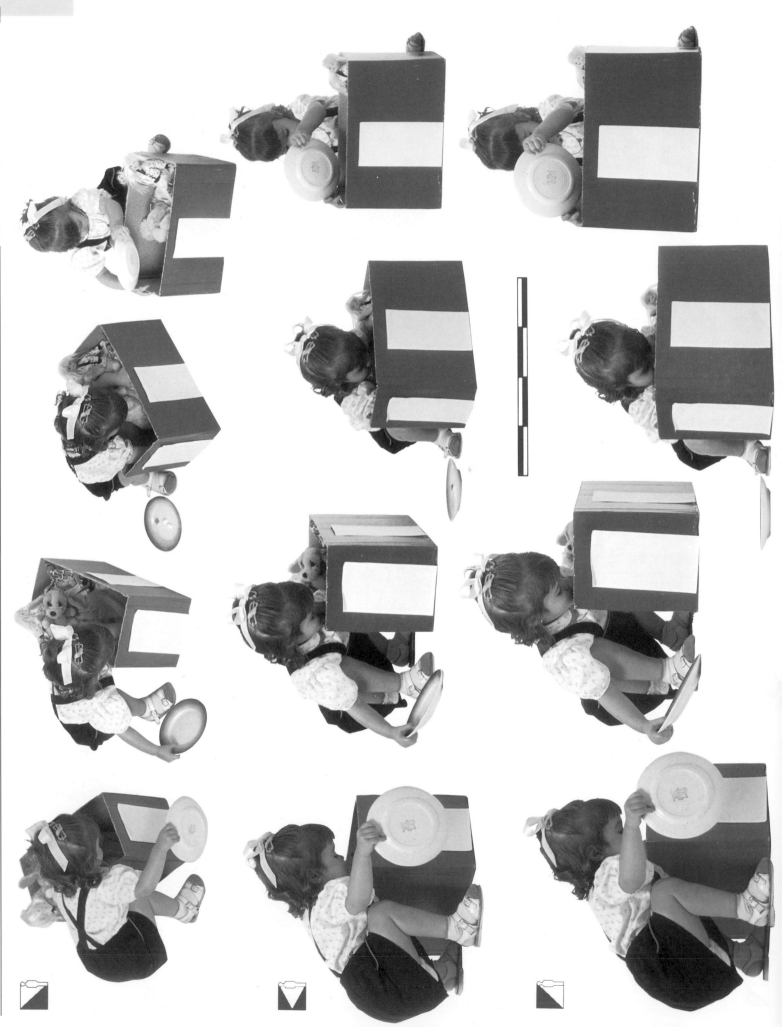

A box of surprises

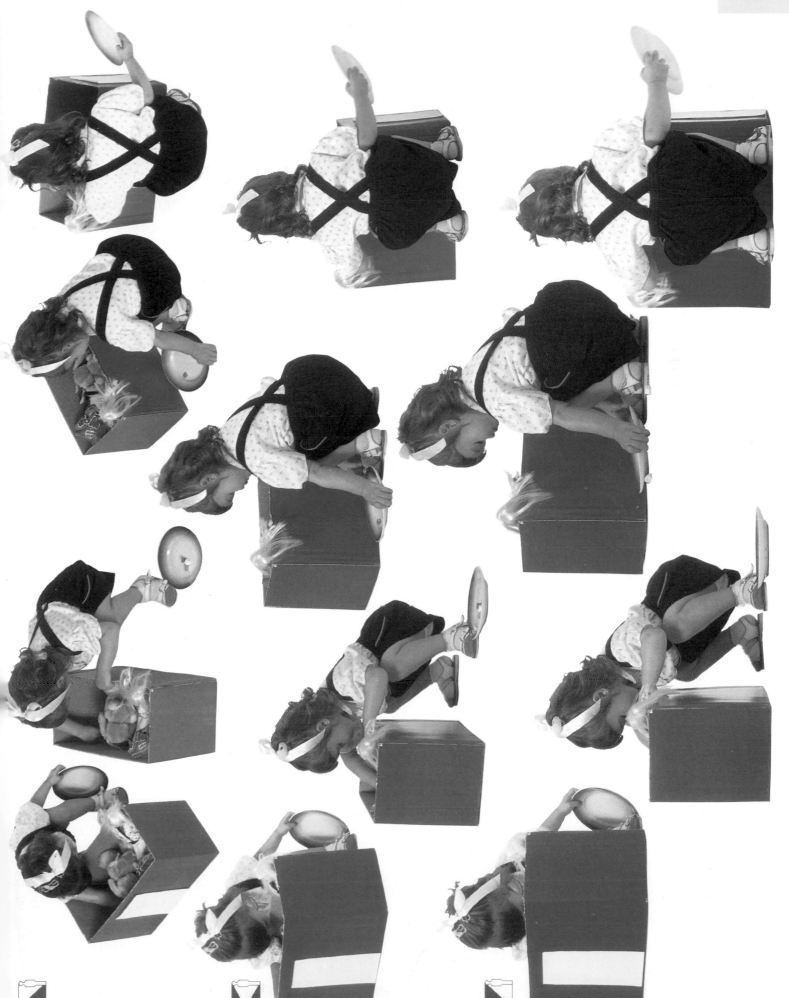

Enjoying a book

Enjoying a book

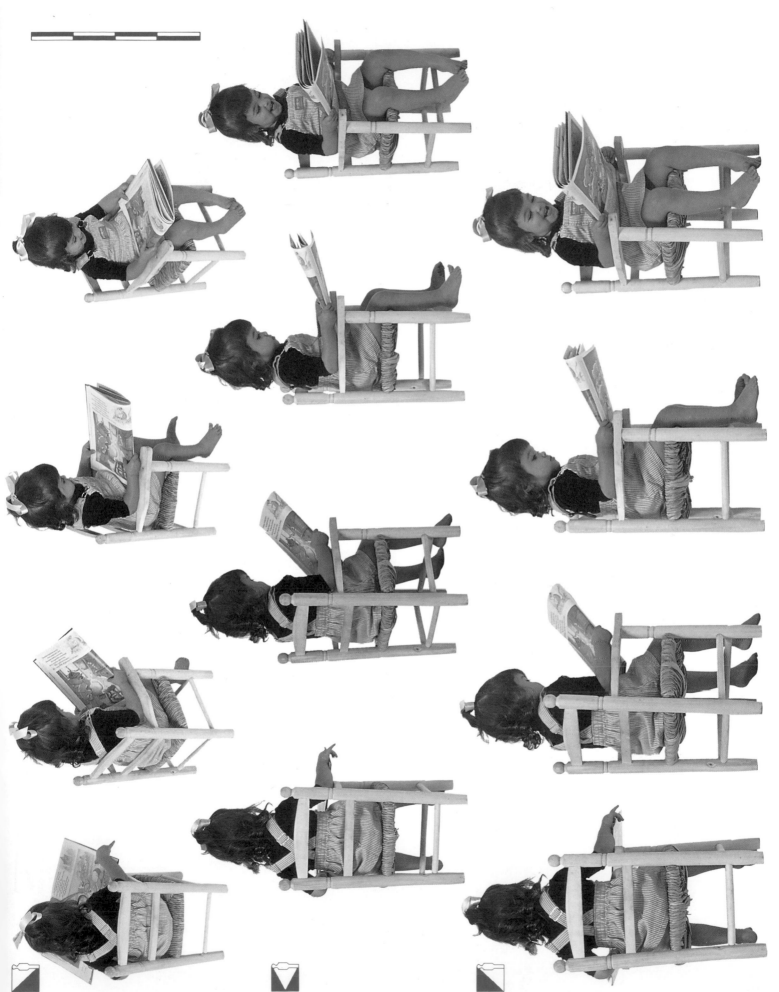

Hello, goodby!

Out in the rain

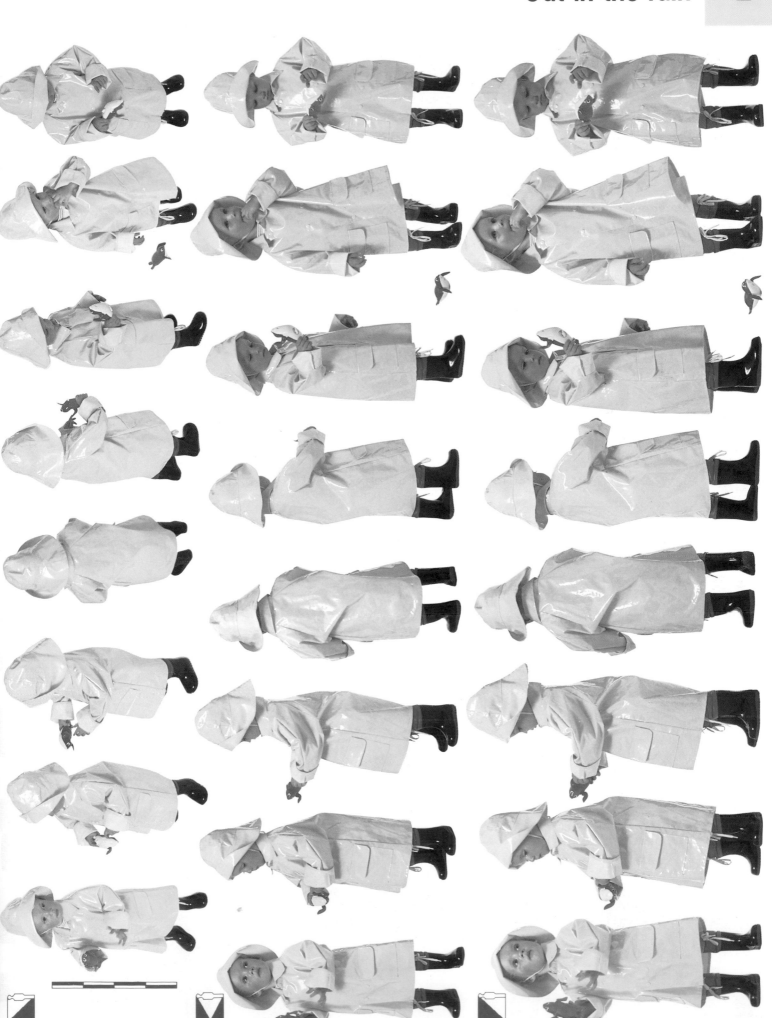

Roughhousing

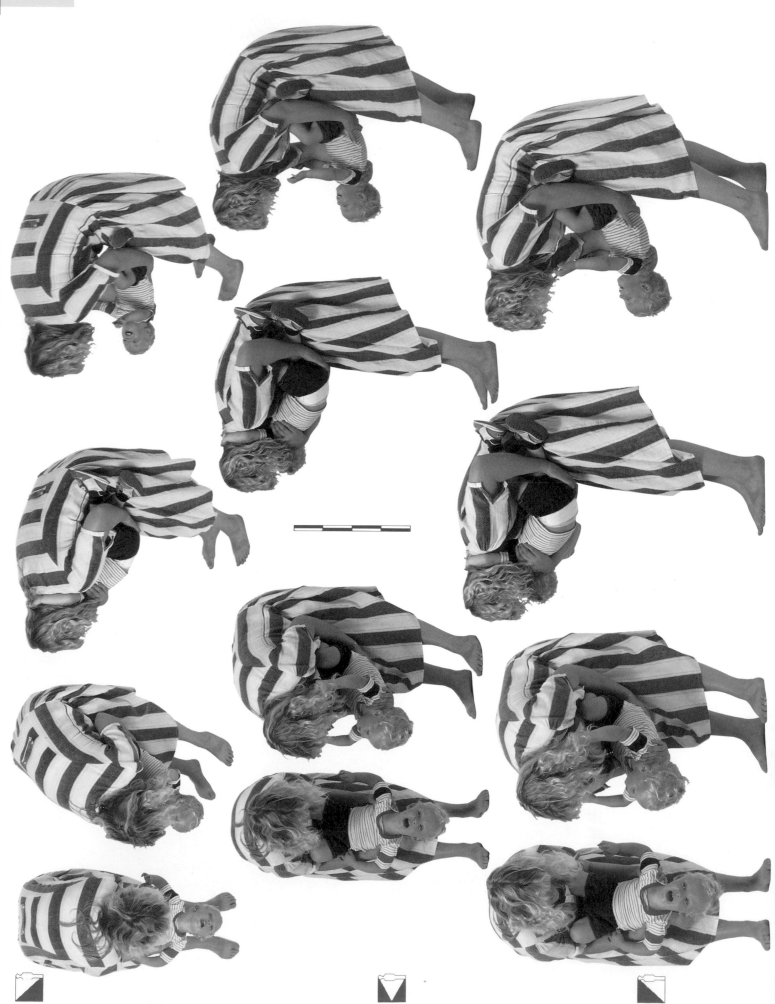

Roughhousing

2·11 # Playing with mum

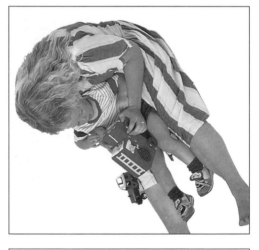

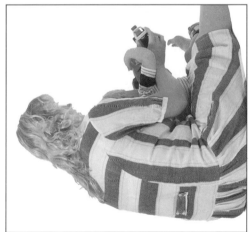

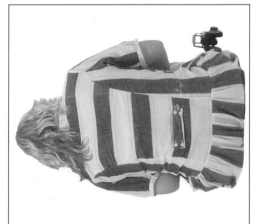
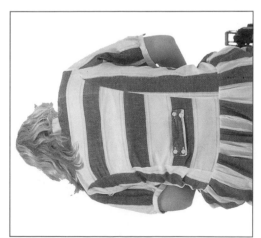

3·01 # Time for a story

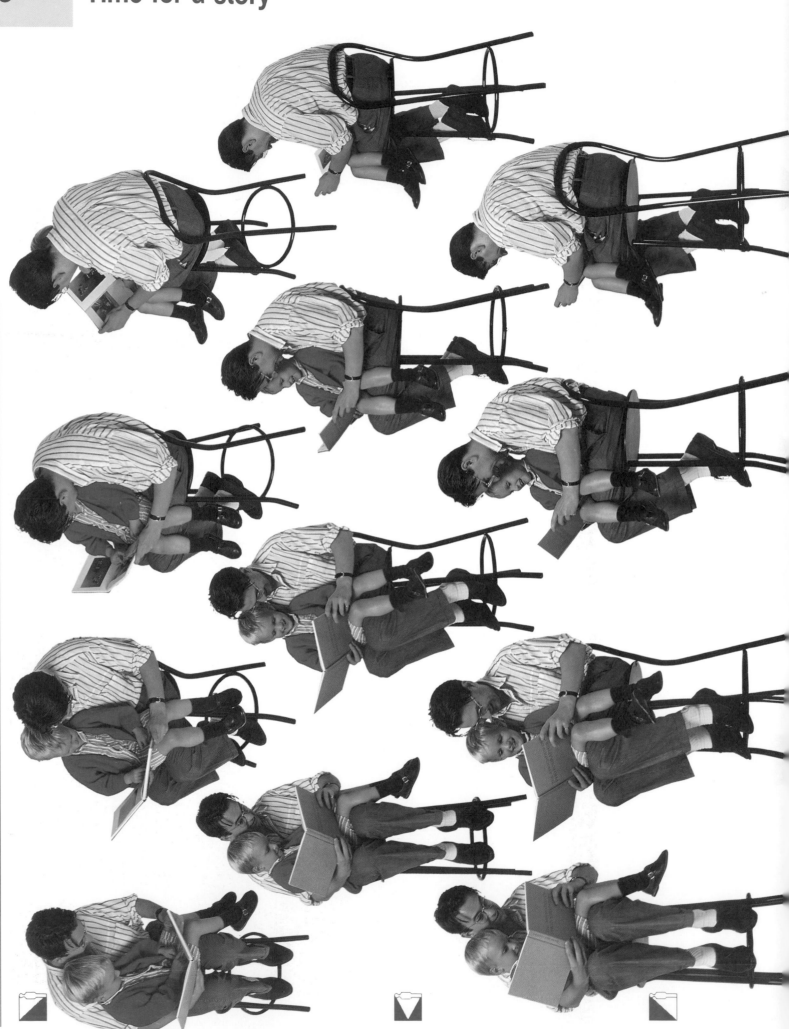

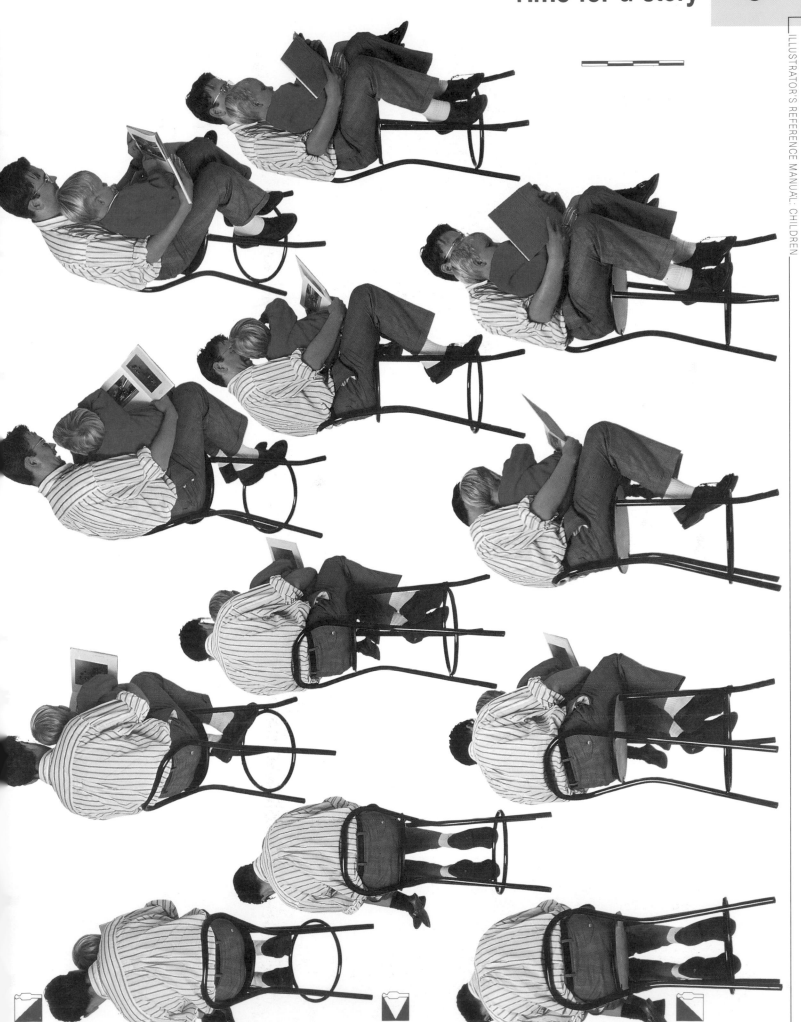

3·02 "Giant's footsteps"

3·03 **Sucking thumb**

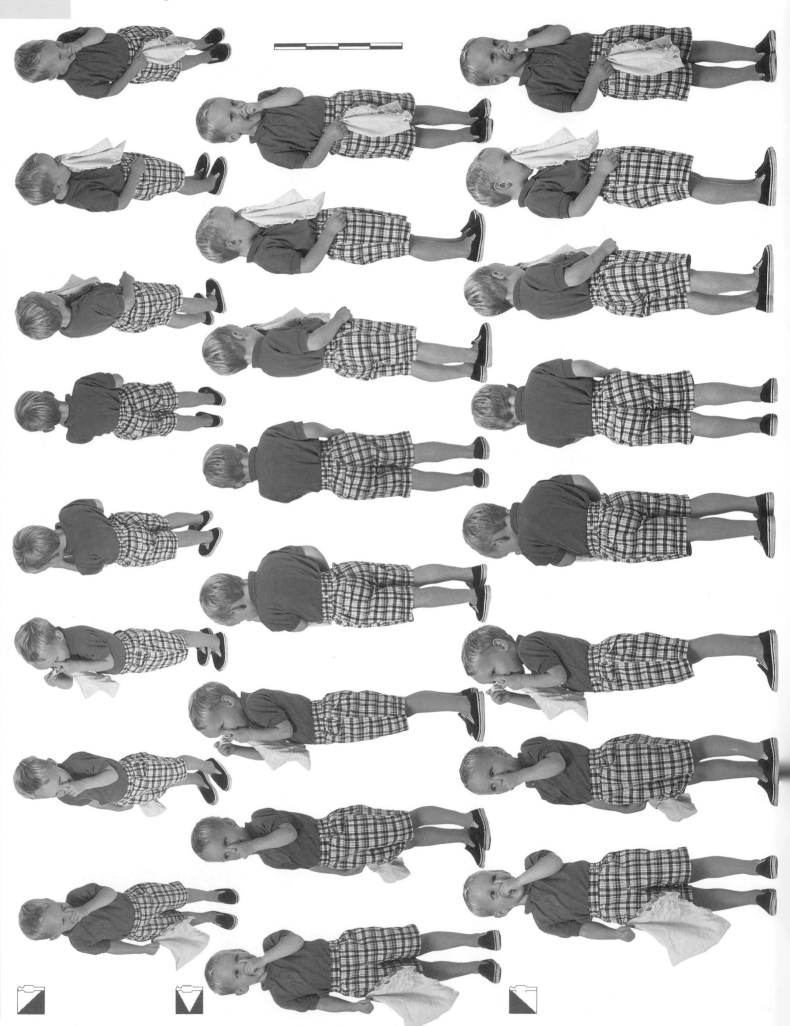

Going swimming

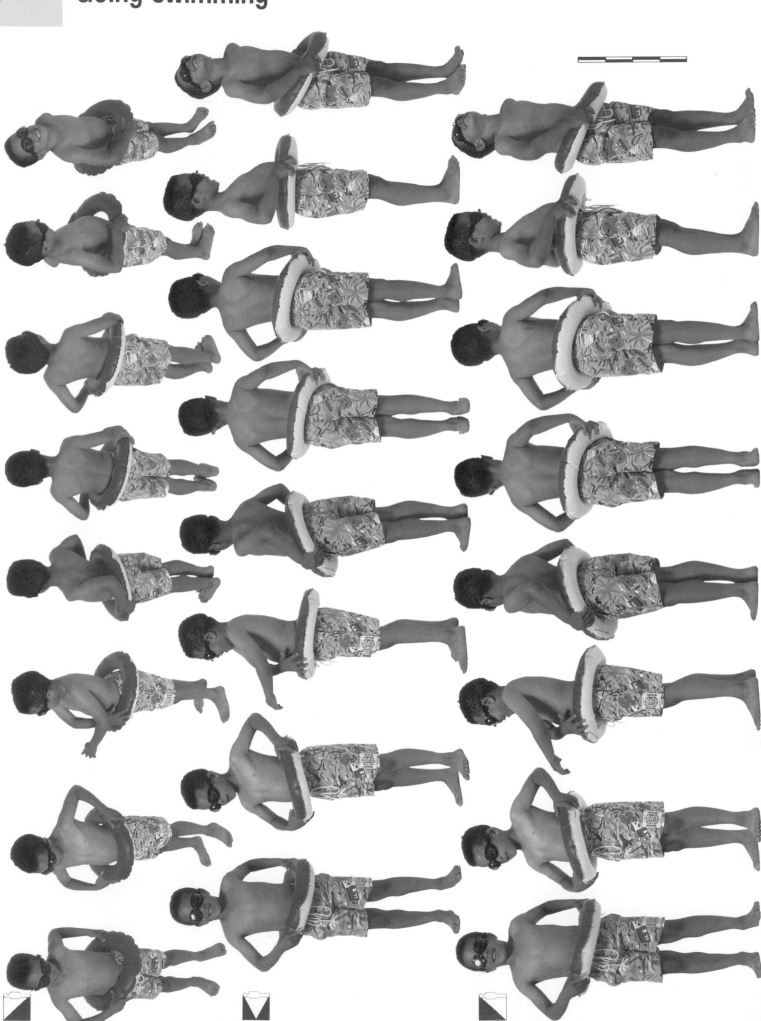

Building a sandcastle

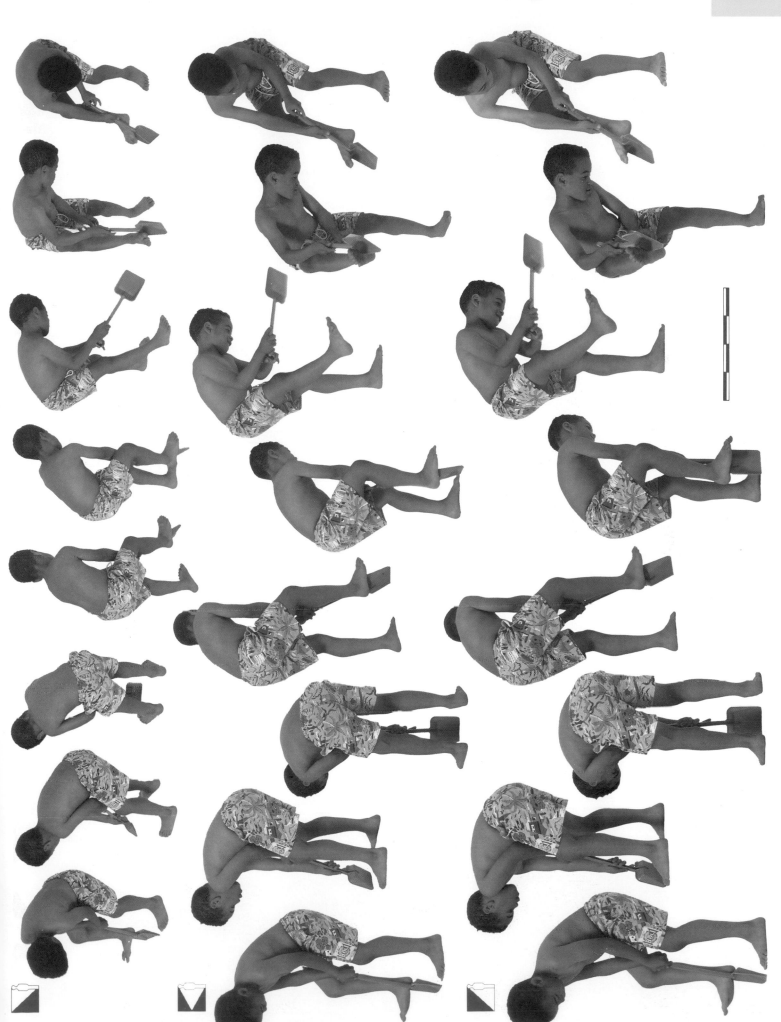

3·07

A new pair of water wings

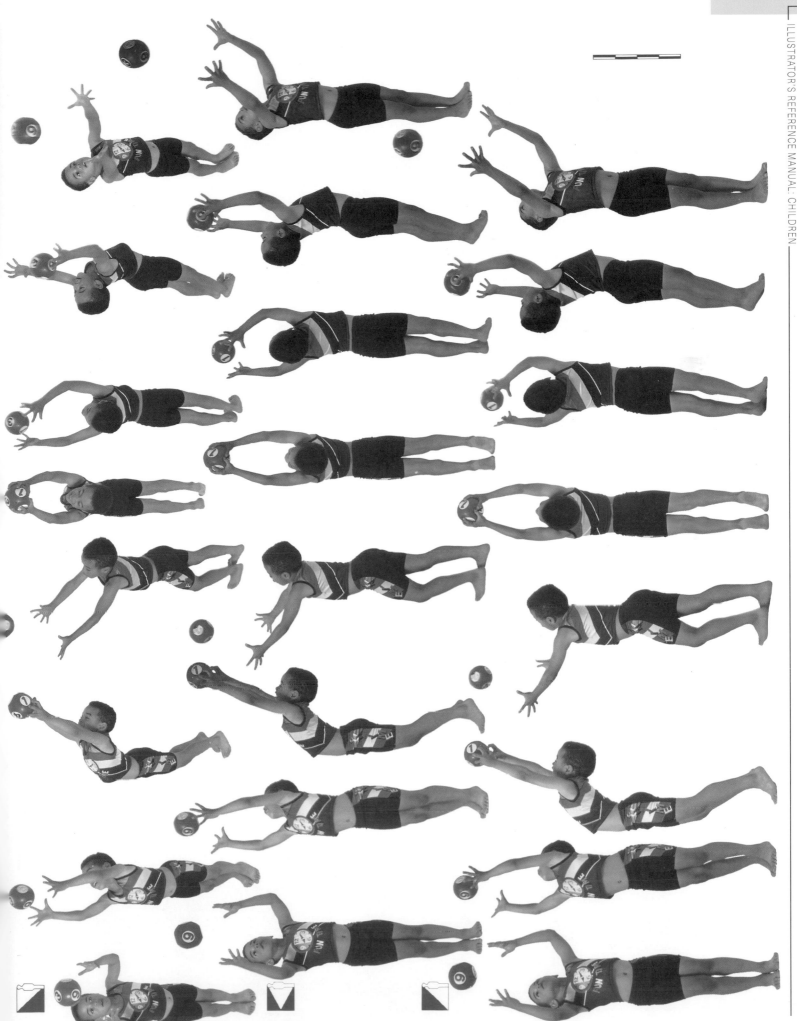

Riding a tricycle

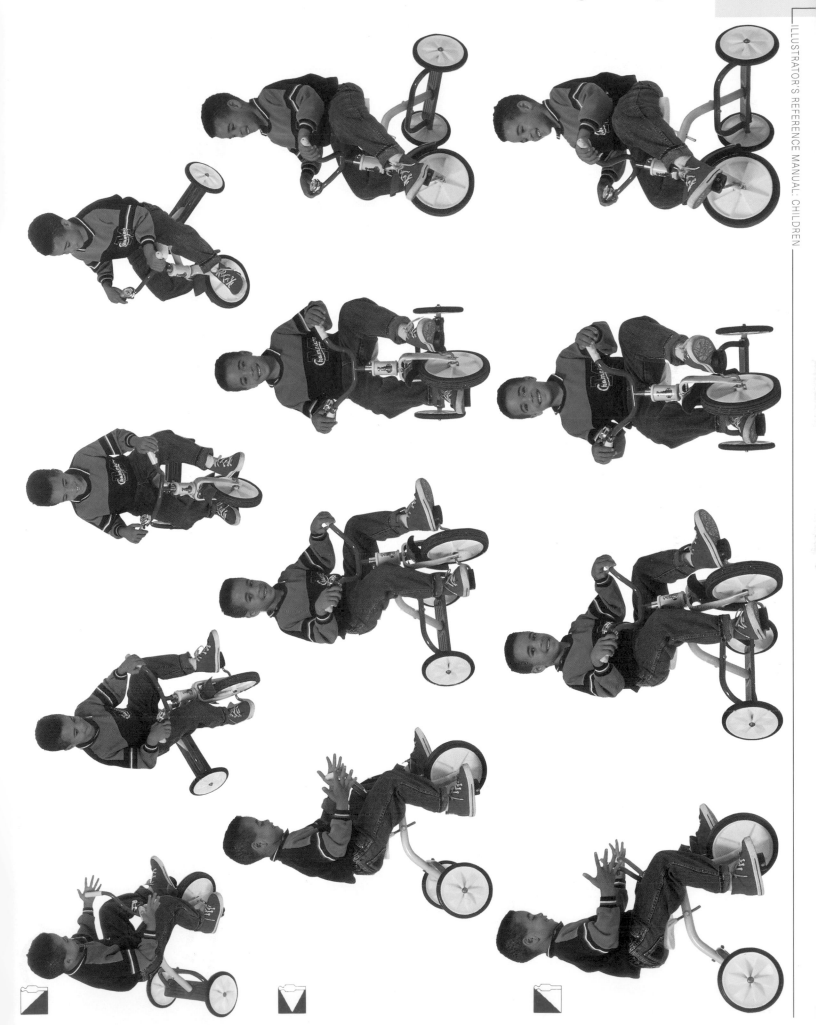

3·10 Making funny faces

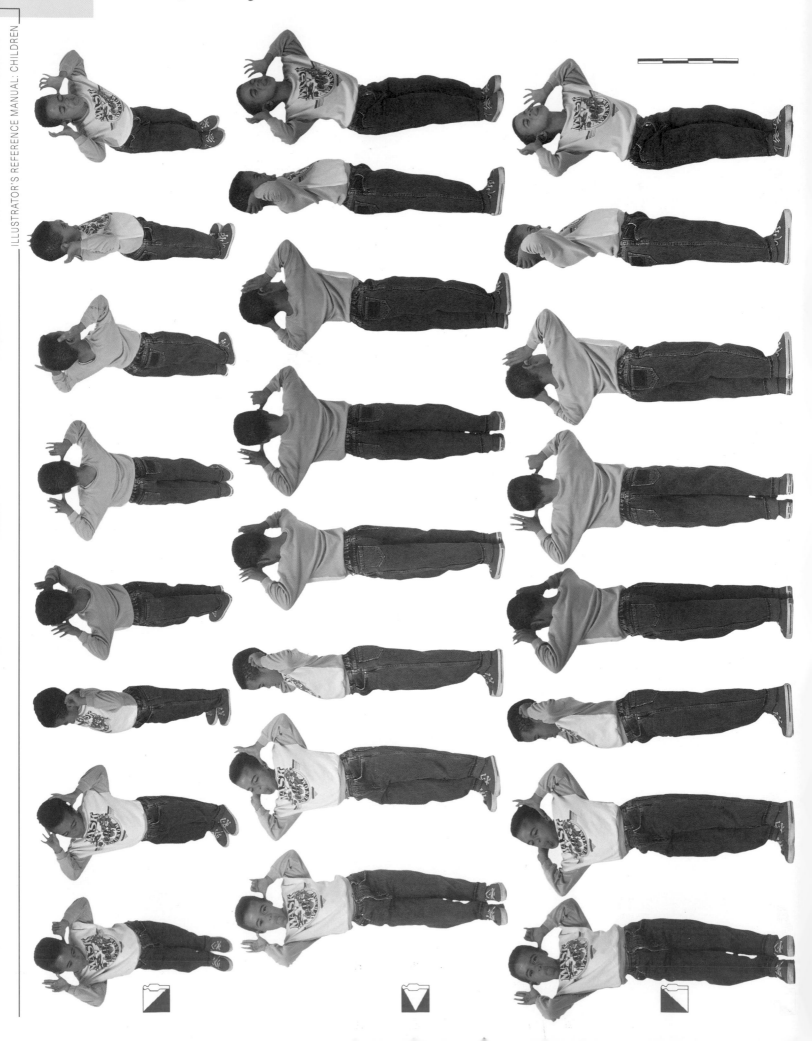

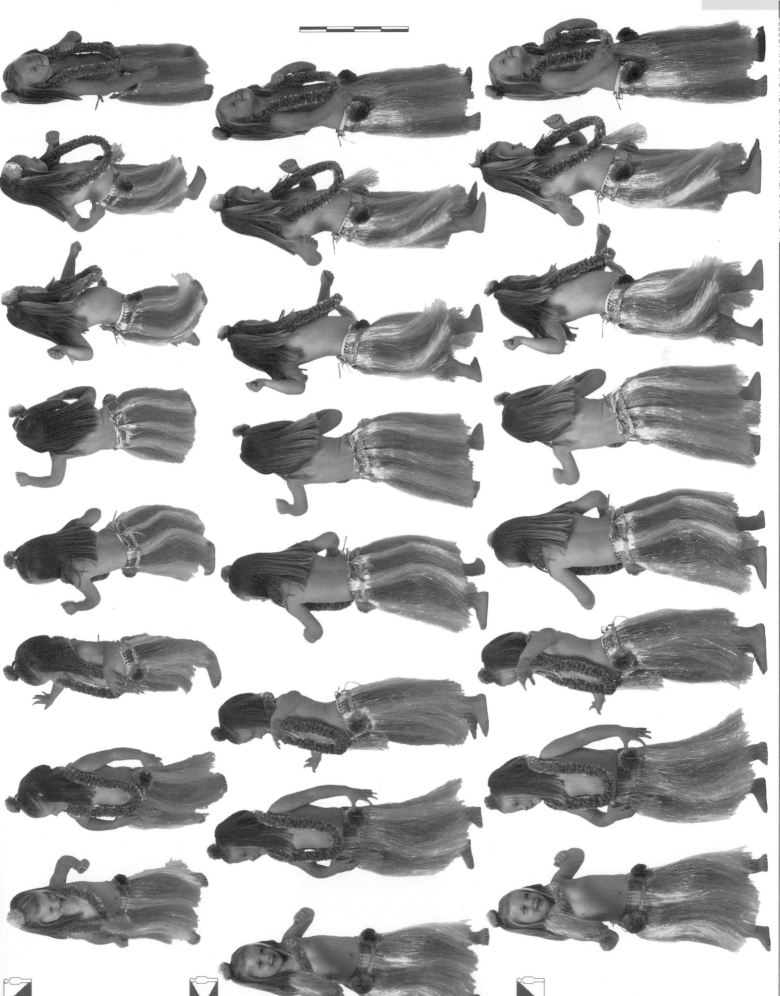

Spiderman – to the rescue!

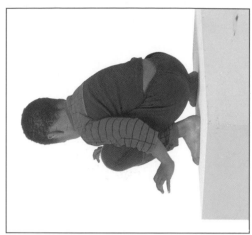

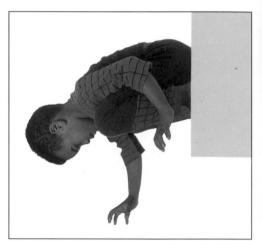

Spiderman – to the rescue!

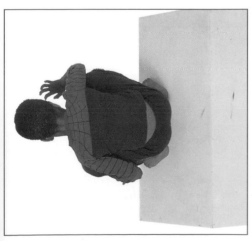

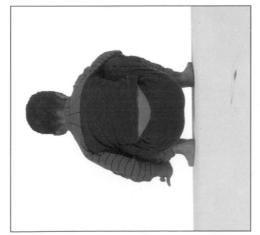

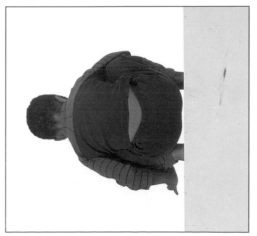

3·13 Hopping

Painting a picture

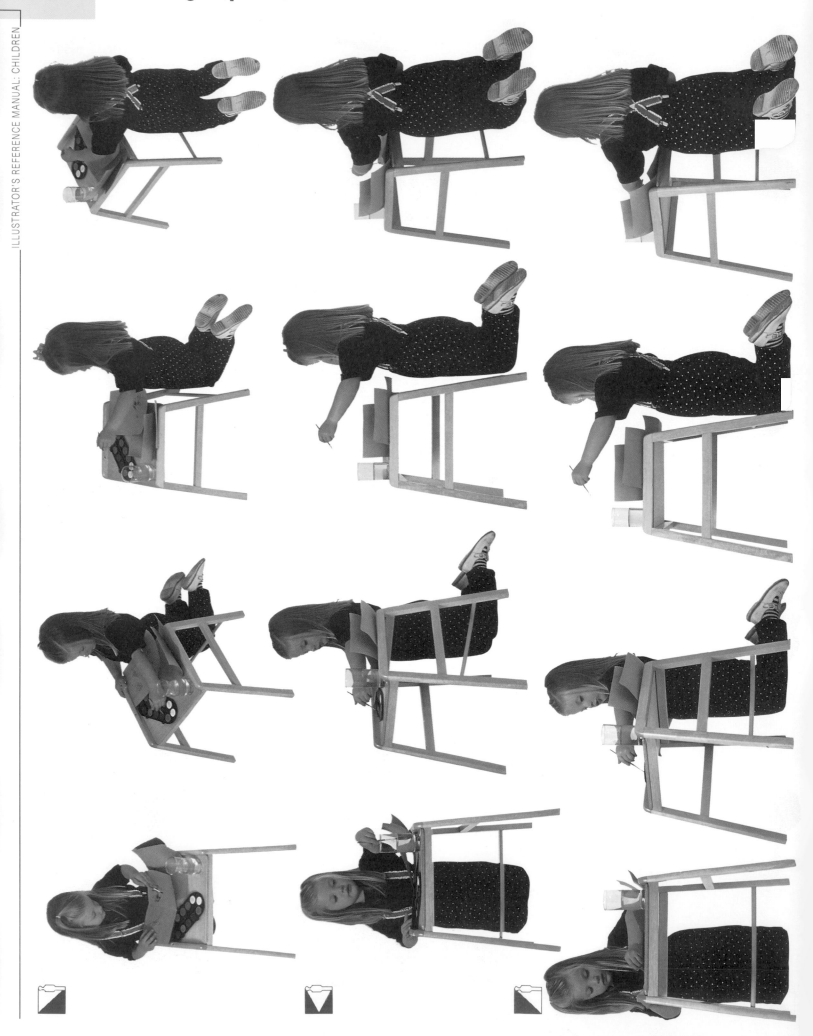

Painting a picture

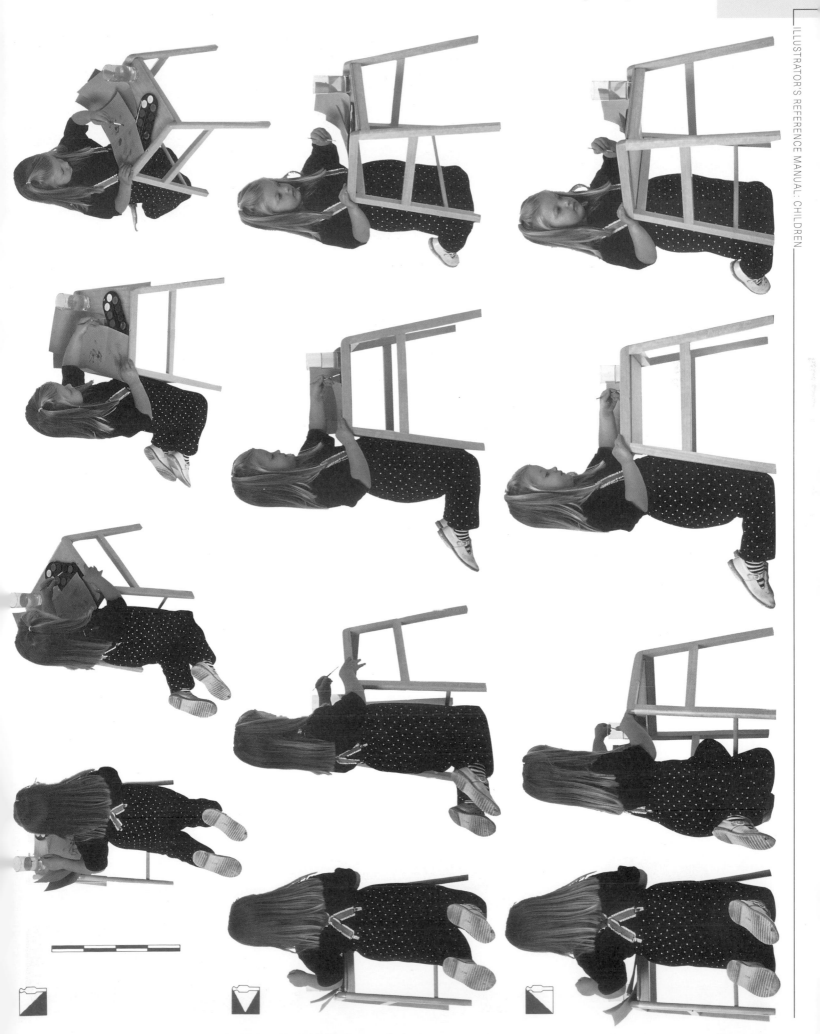

3·16

Playing with toy bus

3·18 Boy and his dog

On adult's shoulders

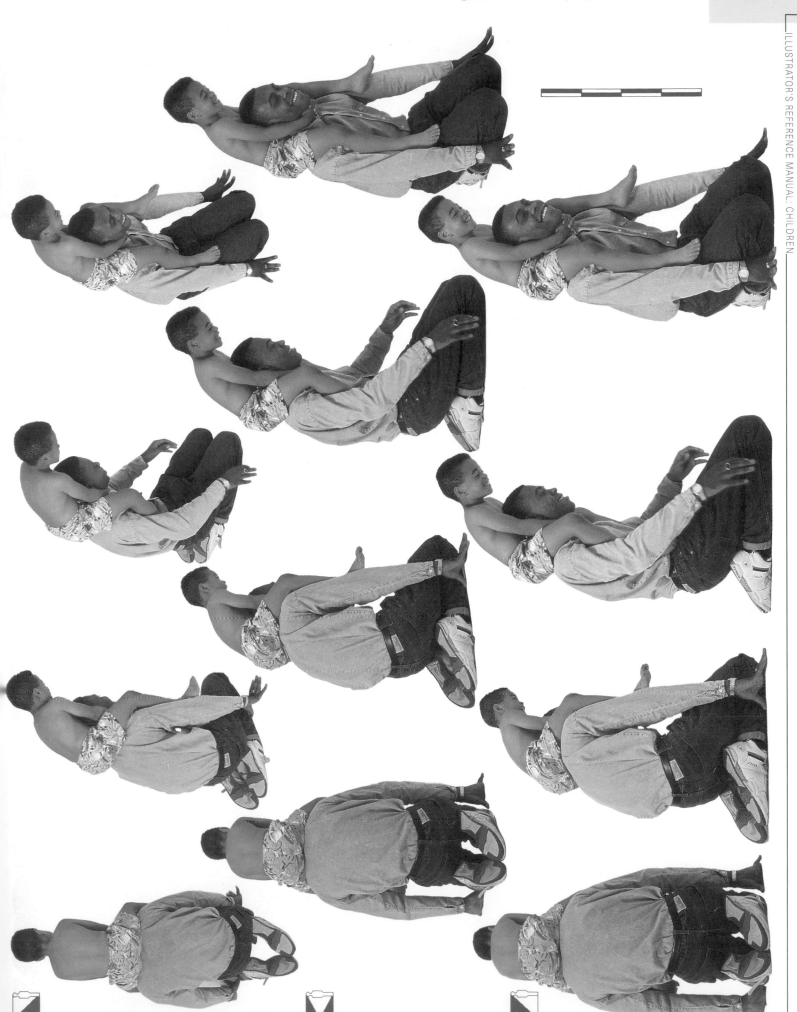

3·20 Carrying a huge cushion

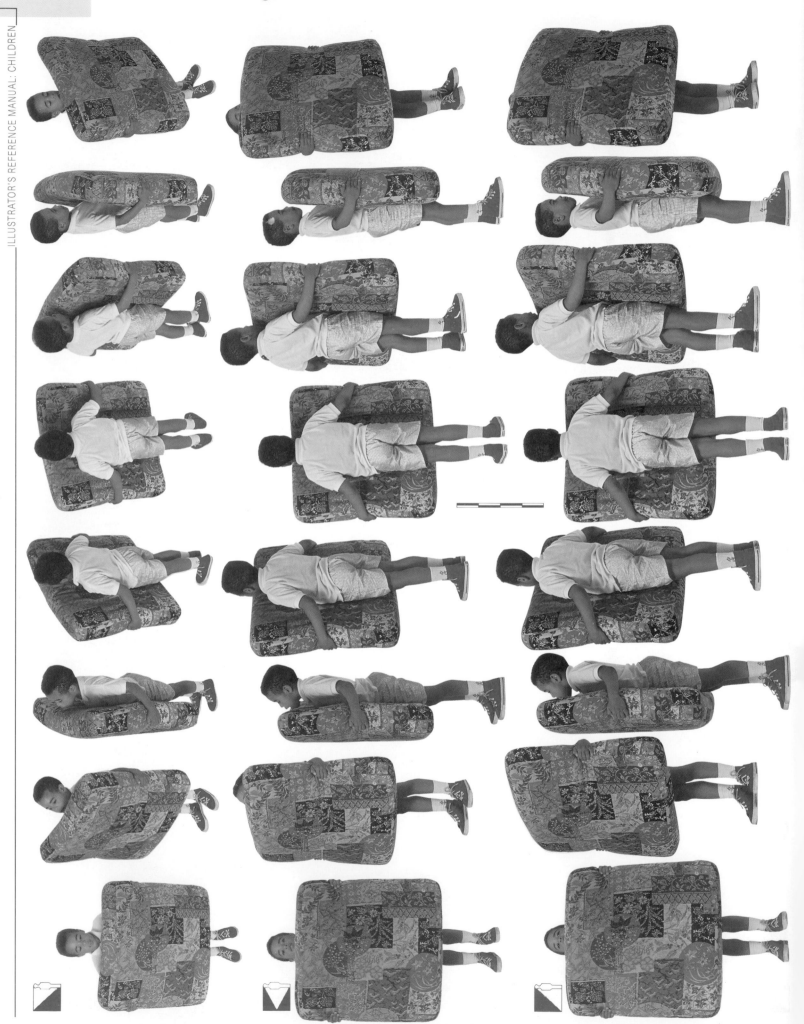

Ready for bed

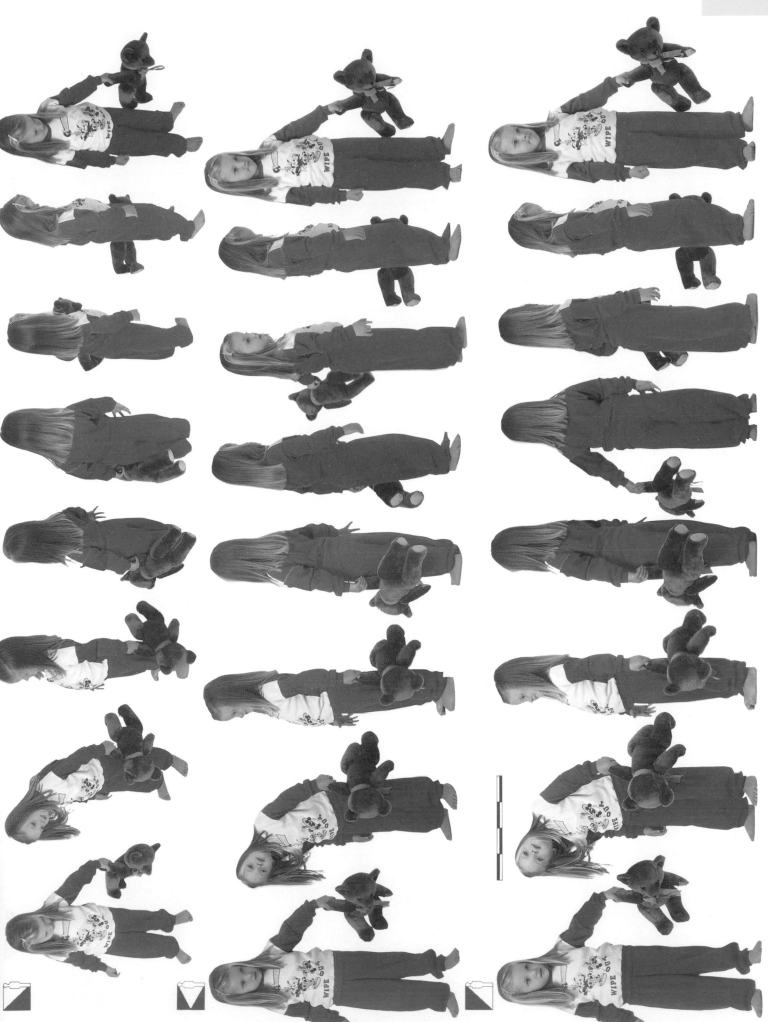

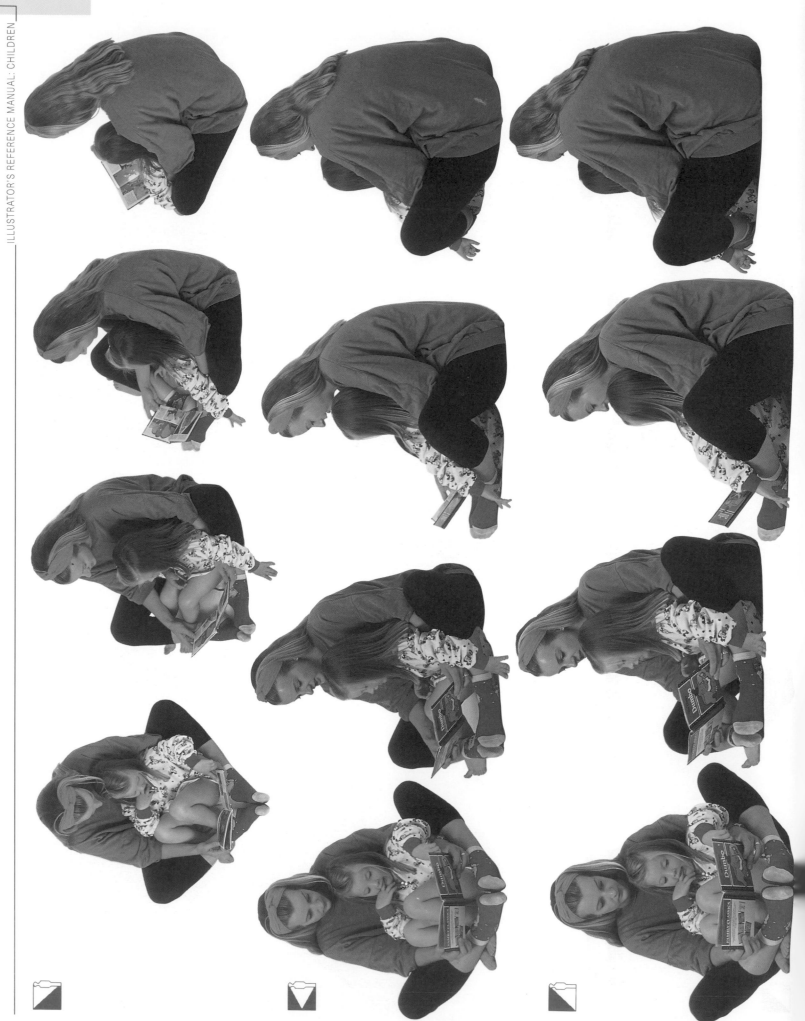

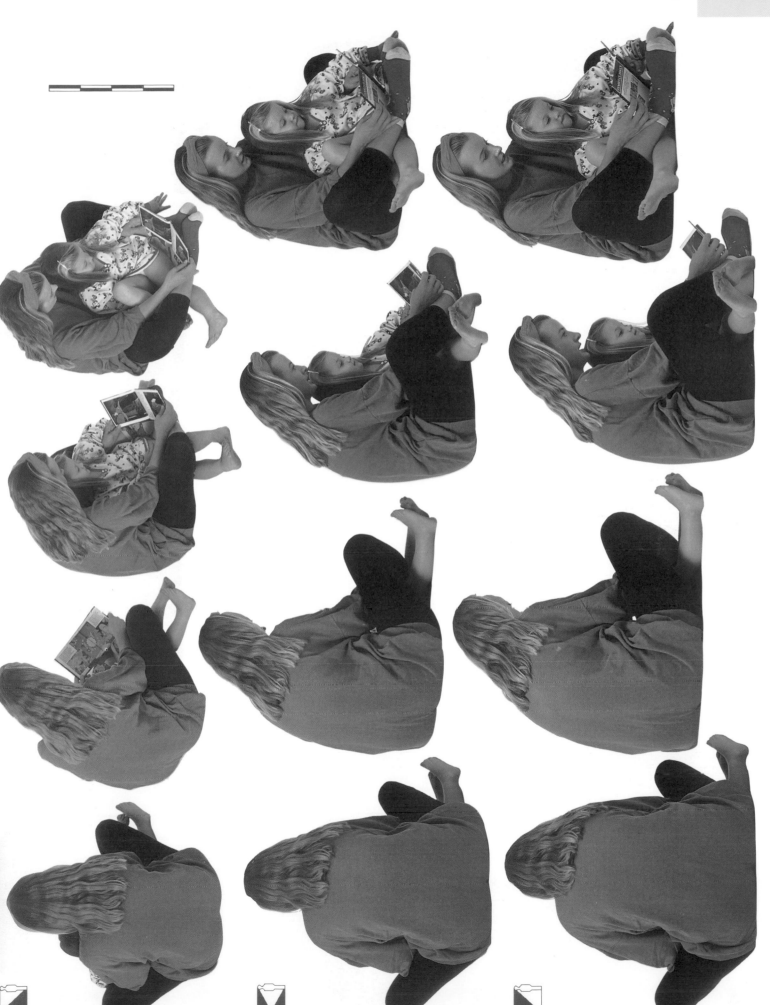

4·01

Pulling on trousers

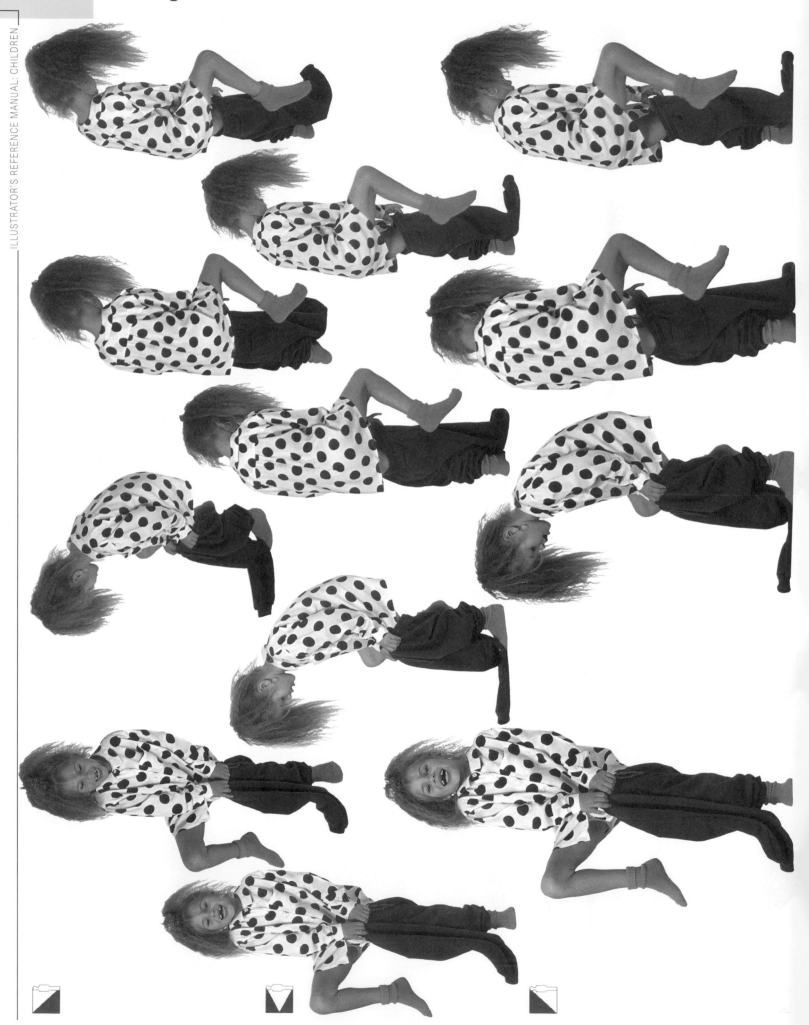

Pulling on trousers

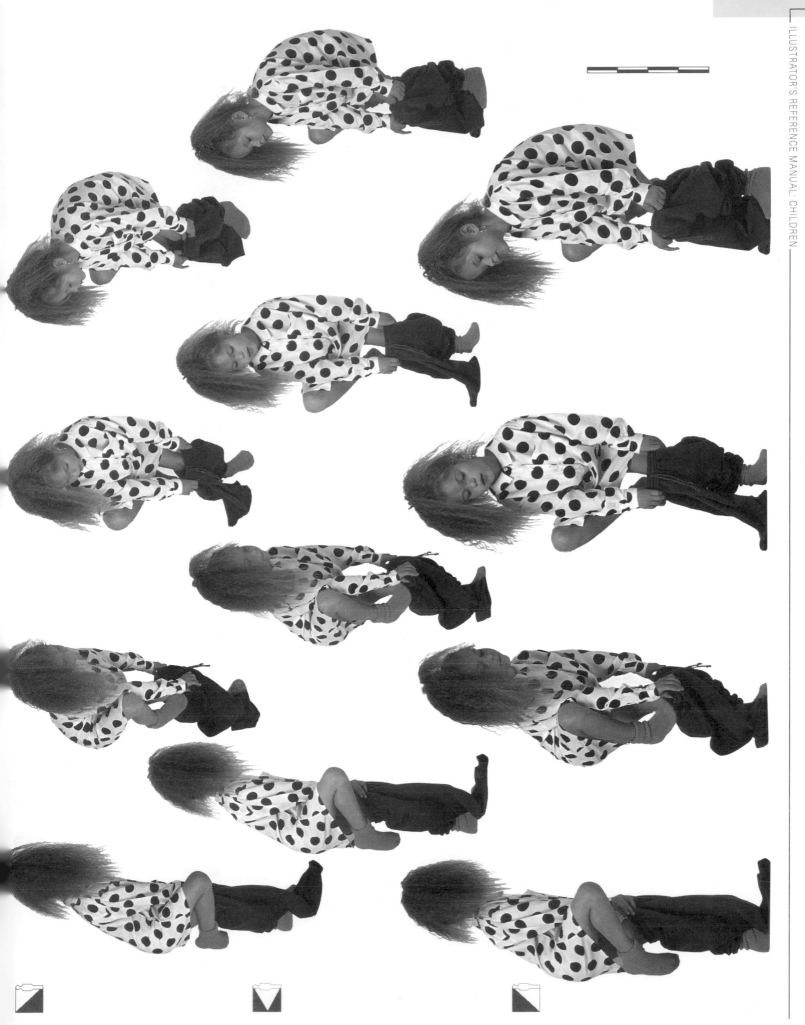

4·02 # Putting on boots

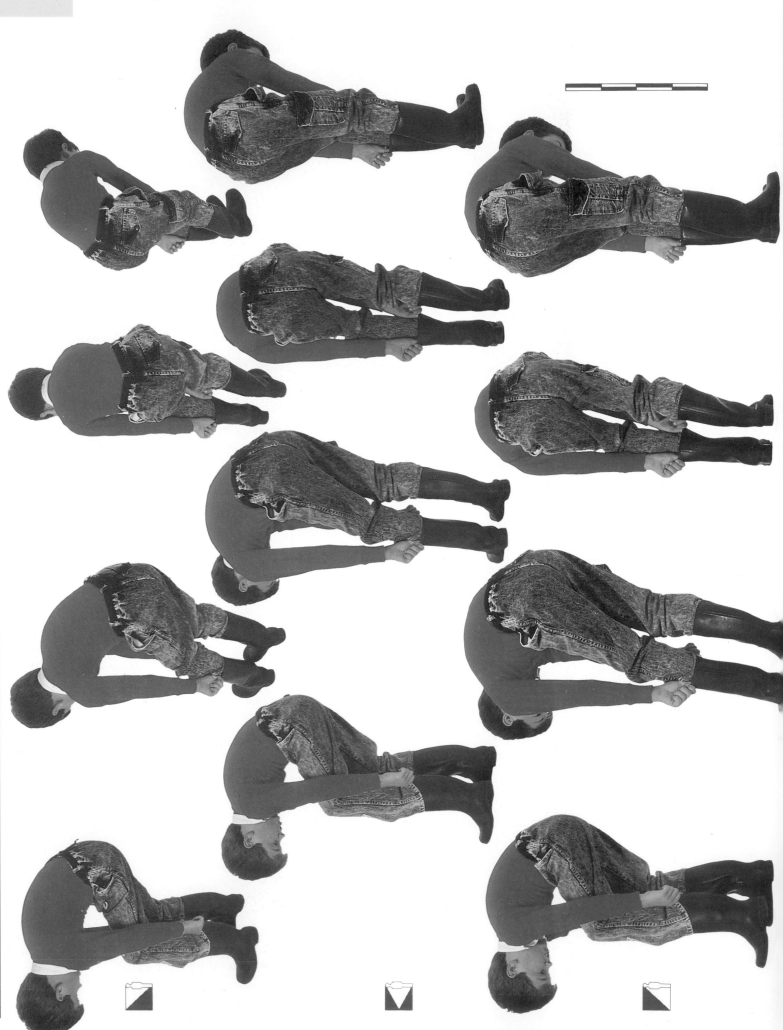

Pulling on boots

Pulling on boots

4·04 Putting on winter coat

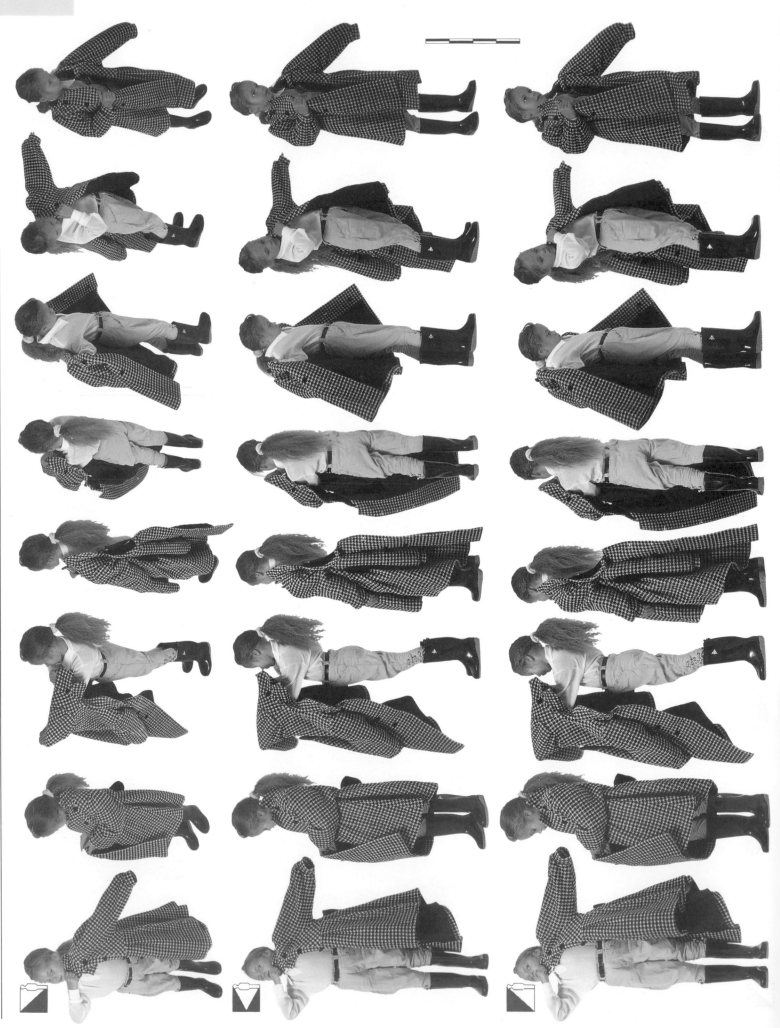

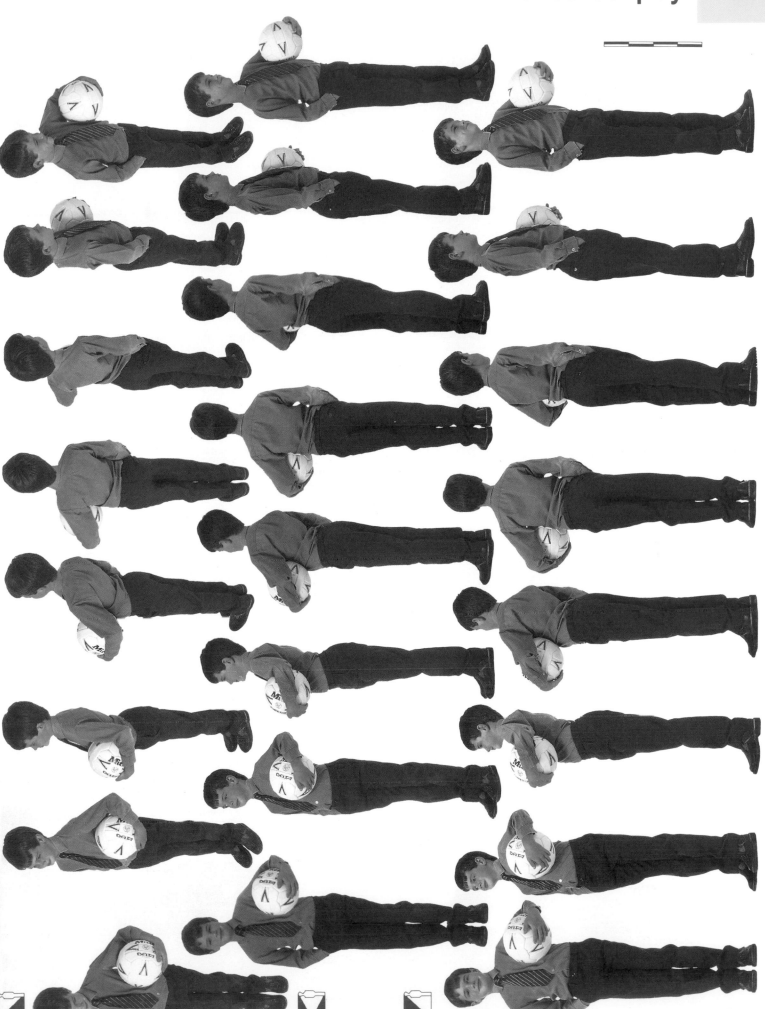

4·06 Anyone for tennis?

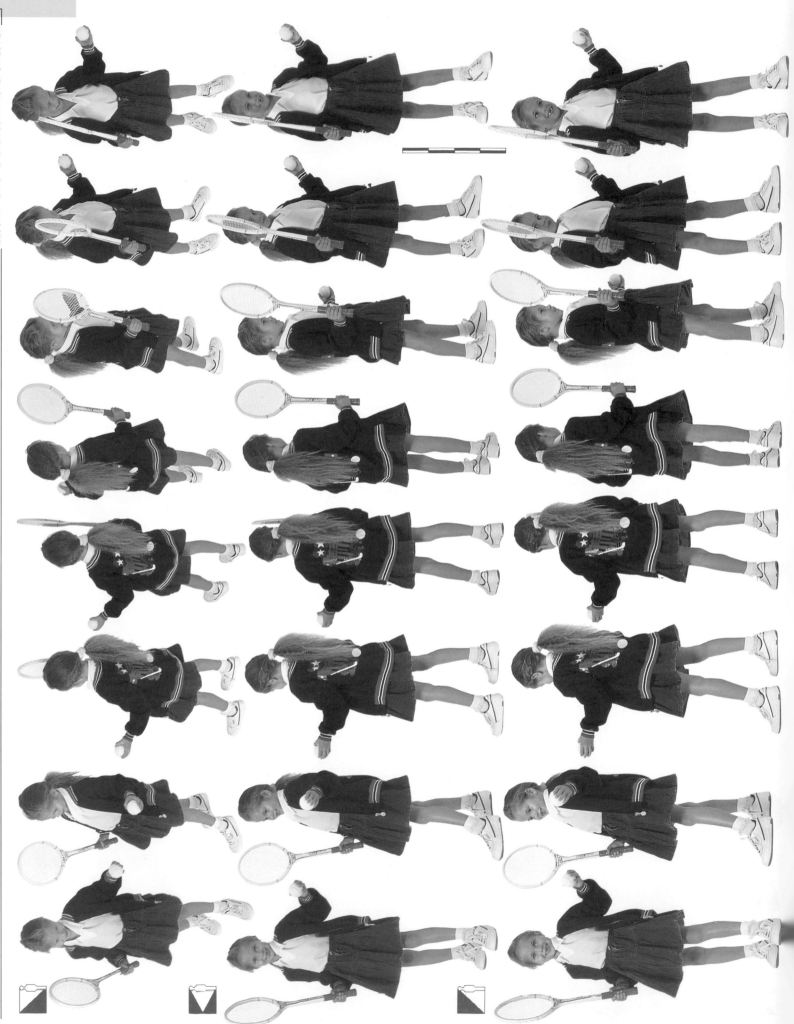

The ballet lesson

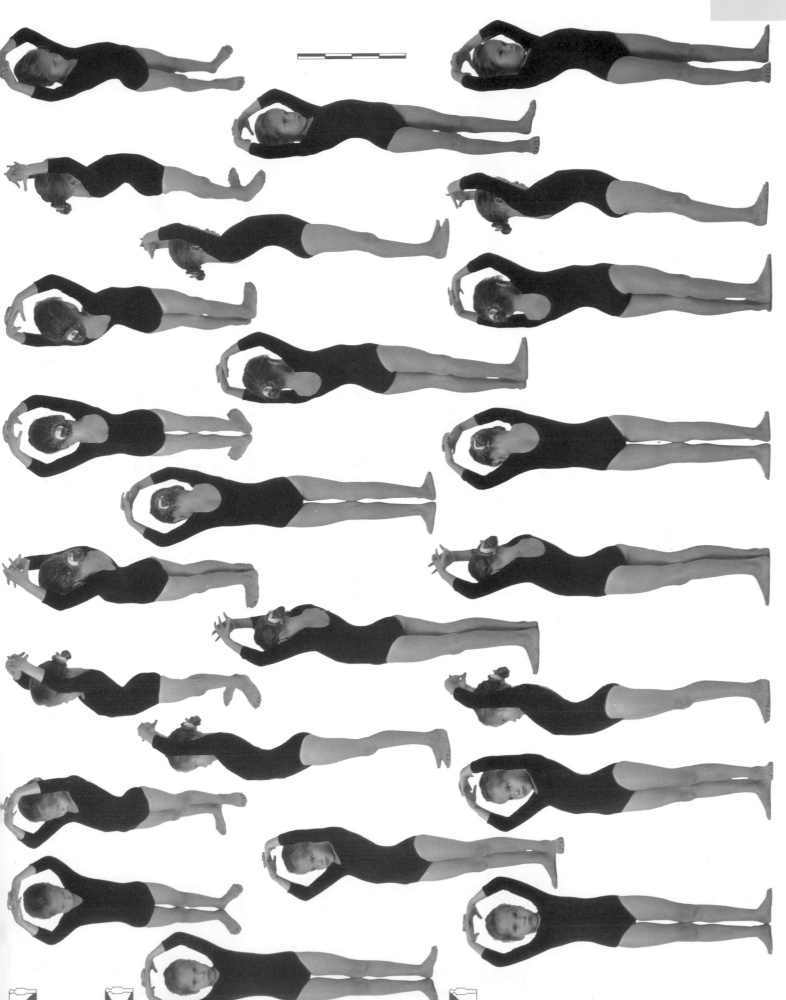

4·08

With plane . . .

. . . Ready for takeoff

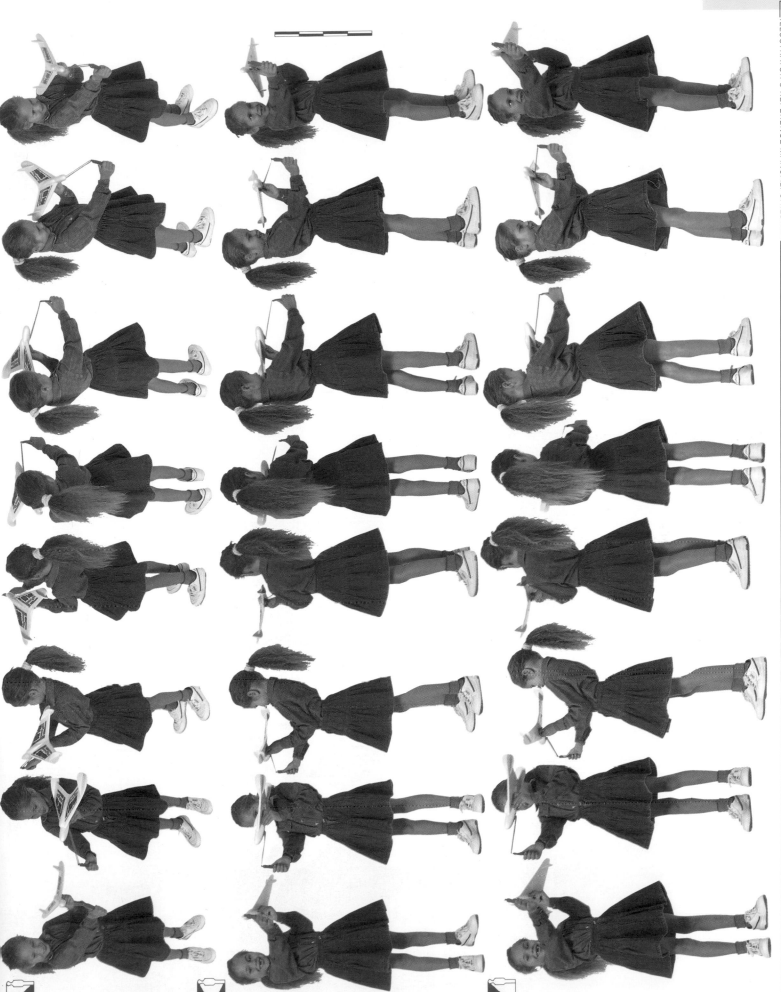

Time for a snack

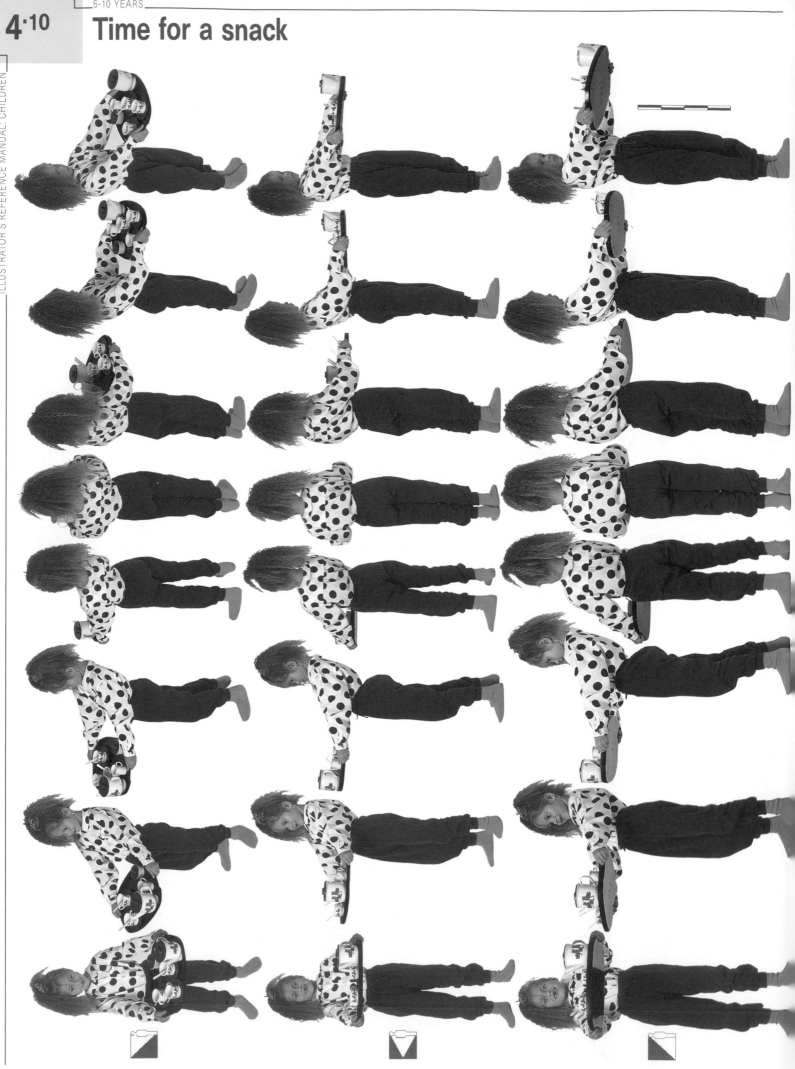

Folding clothes

4·12

Perched on high chair

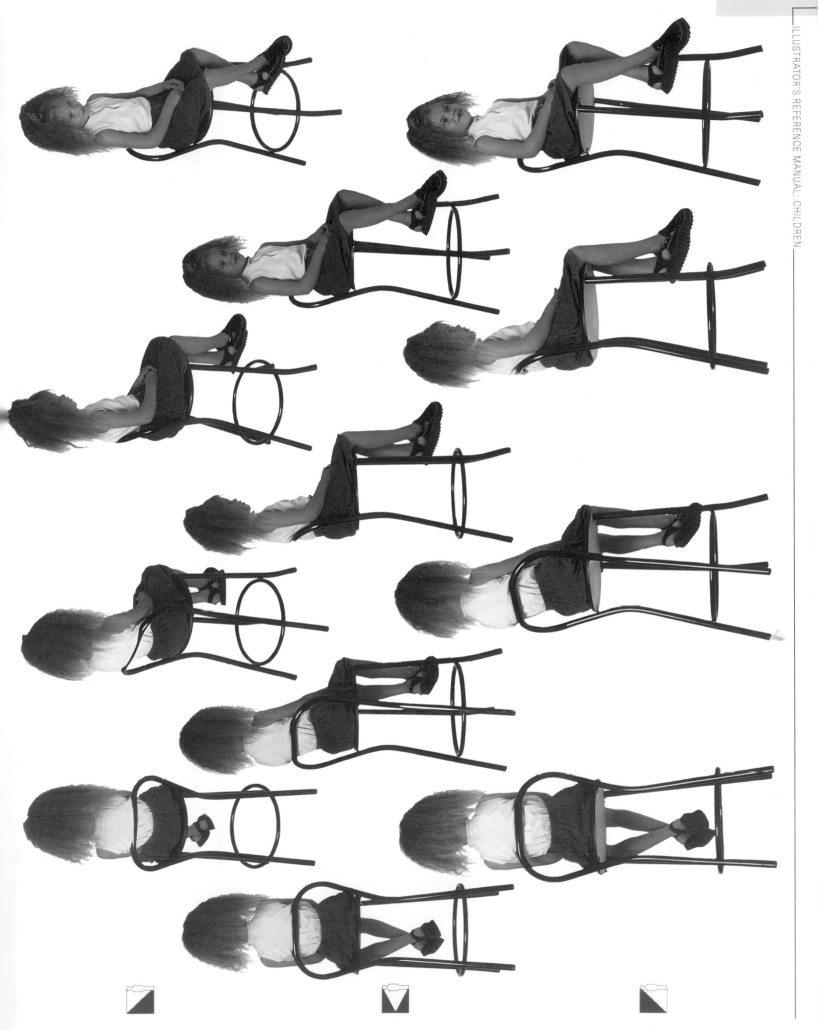

4·13 Playing with construction toy

Playing with construction toy

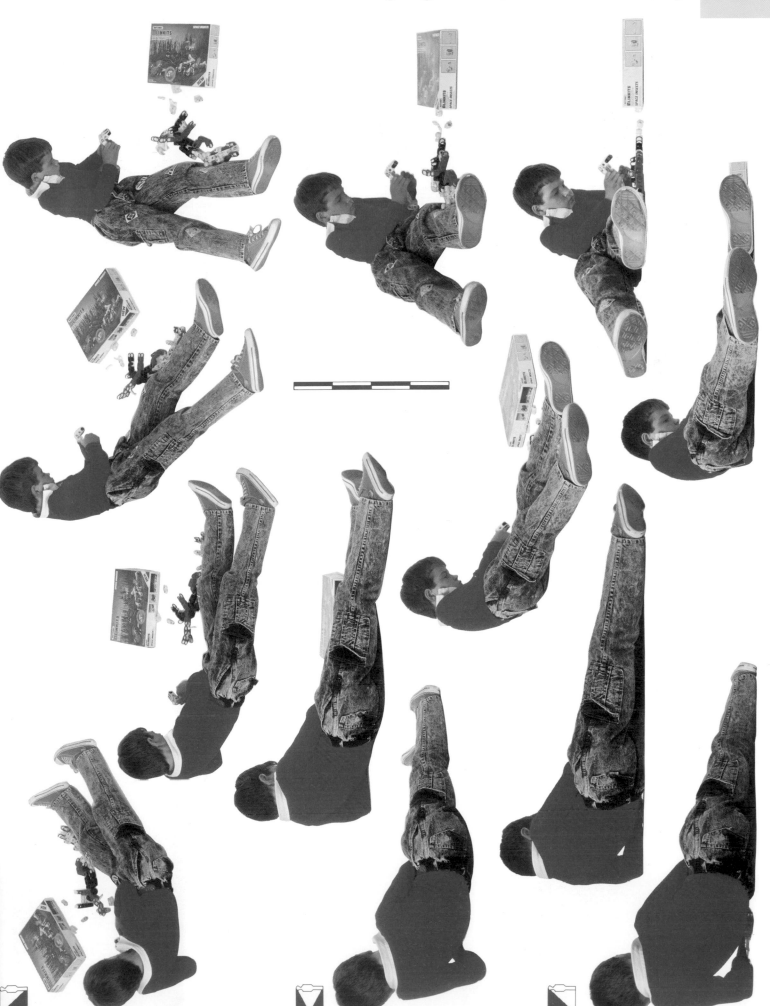

4·14 **Playing with dollhouse**

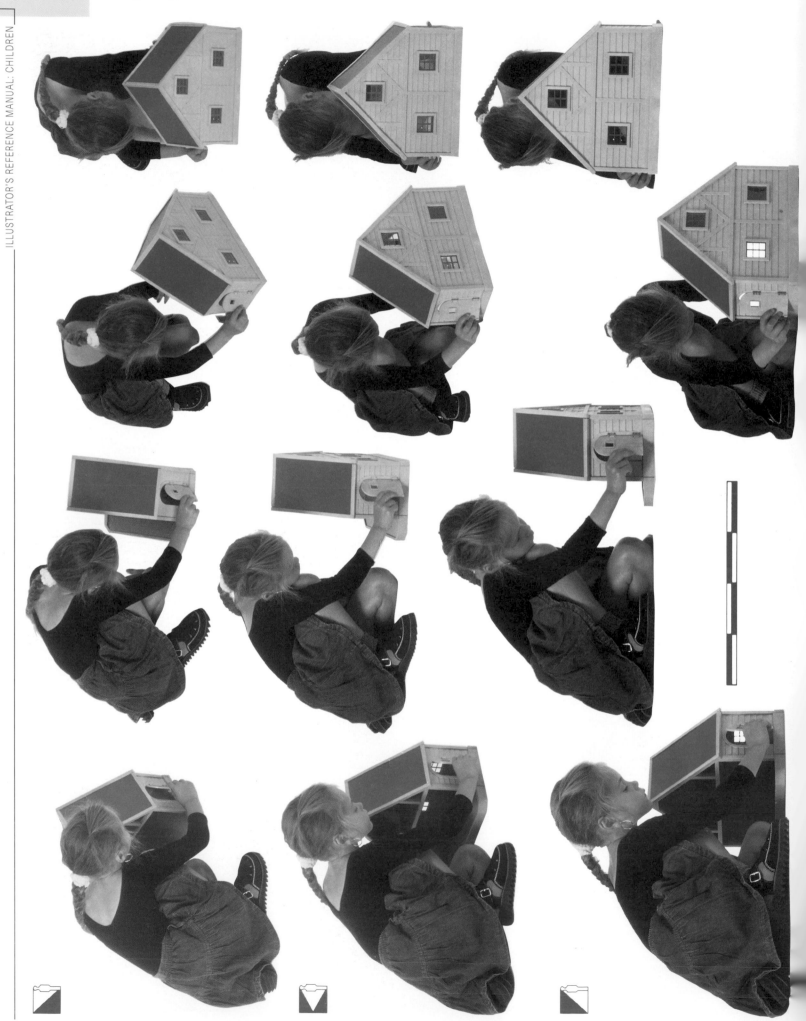

Playing with dollhouse

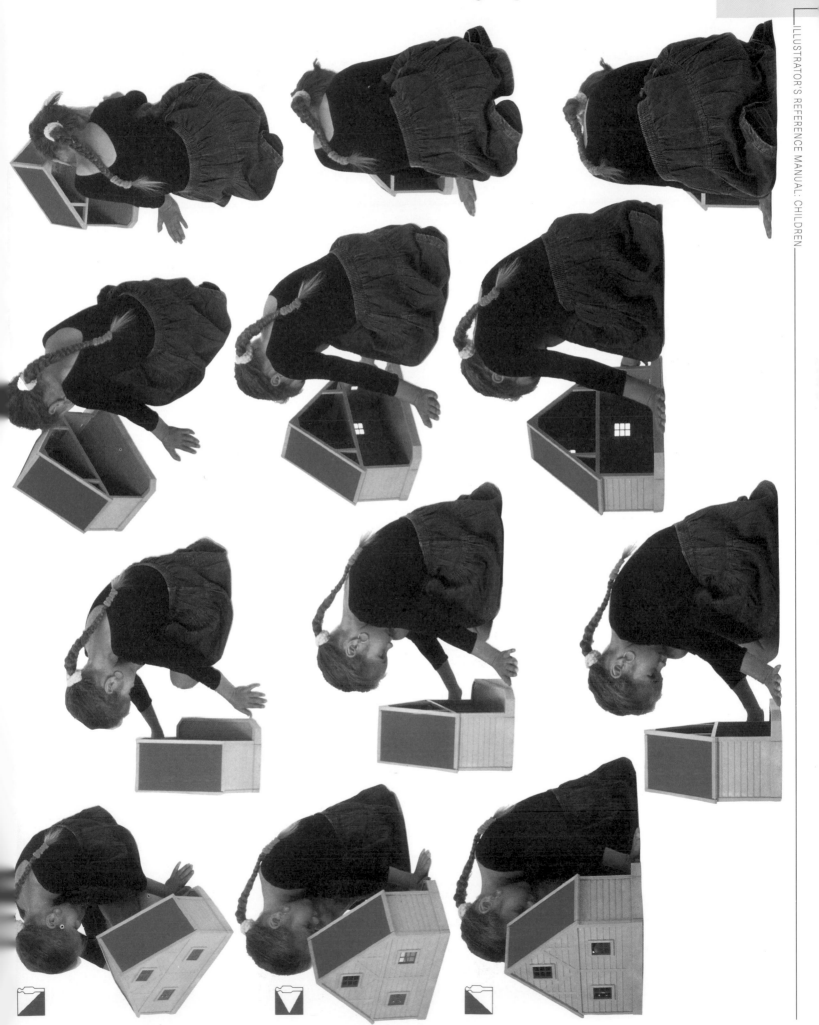

Playing with model car

Lying reading comic

4·17

Sitting reading comic

Sitting reading comic

Sitting on bike

4·18

4·19

To the beach

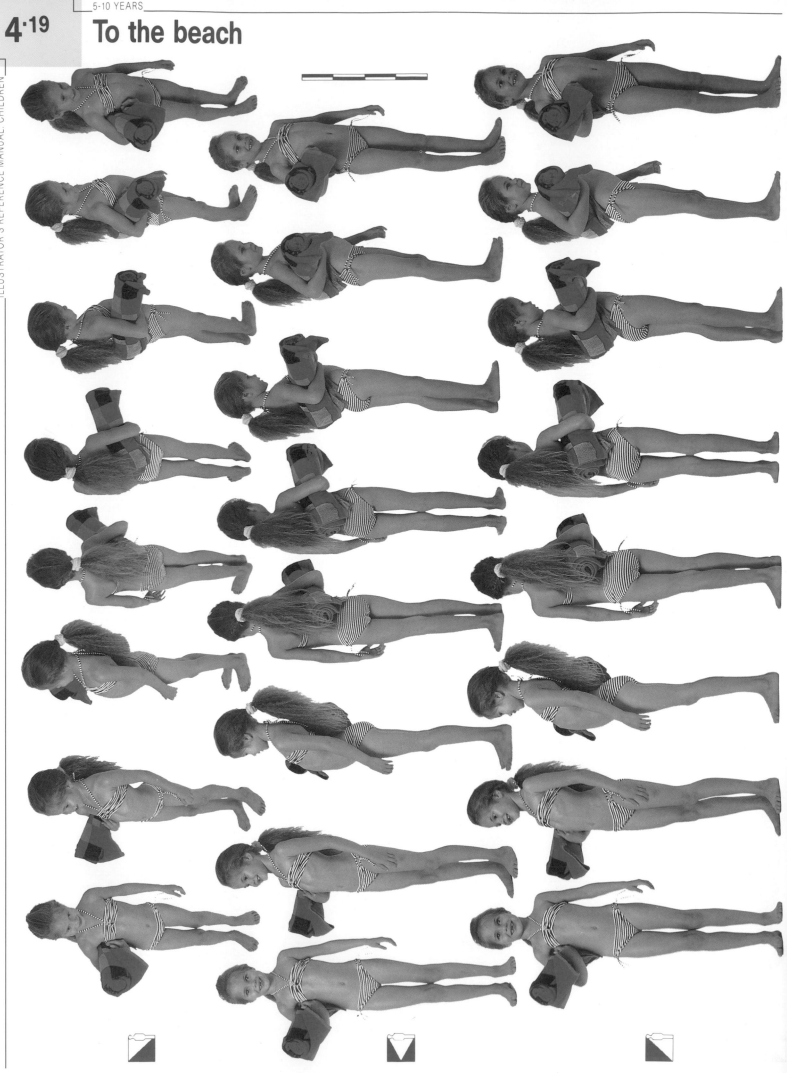

4·21 # Head over heels

Doing a handstand

4·23 Little monster!

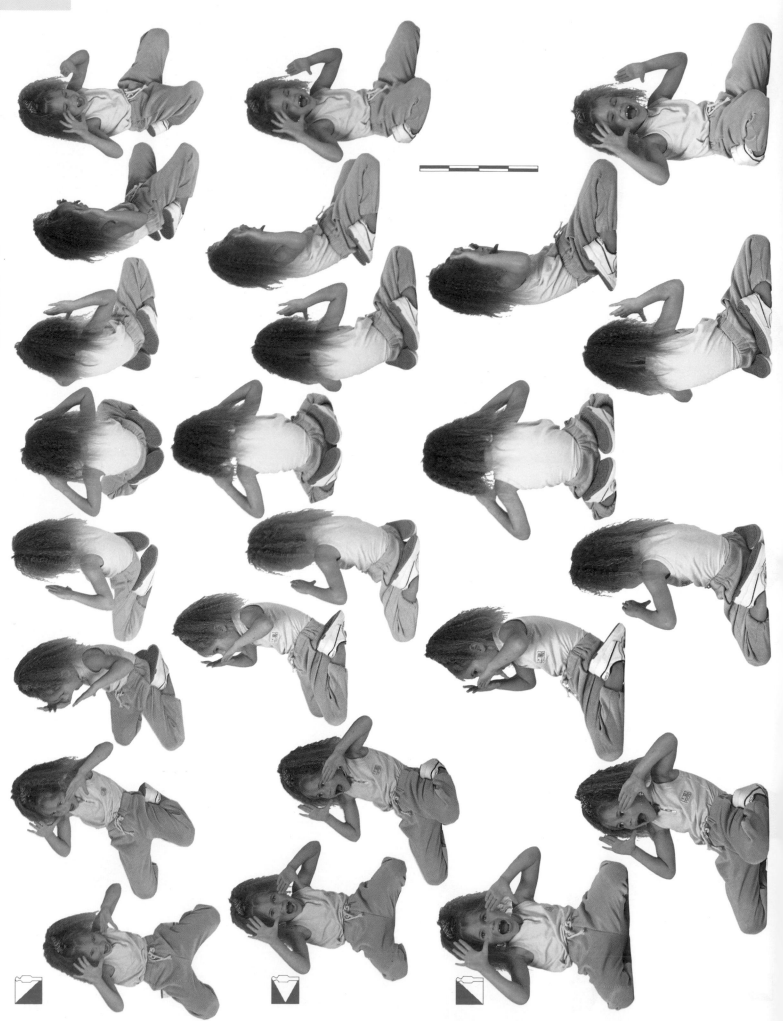

Saying prayers

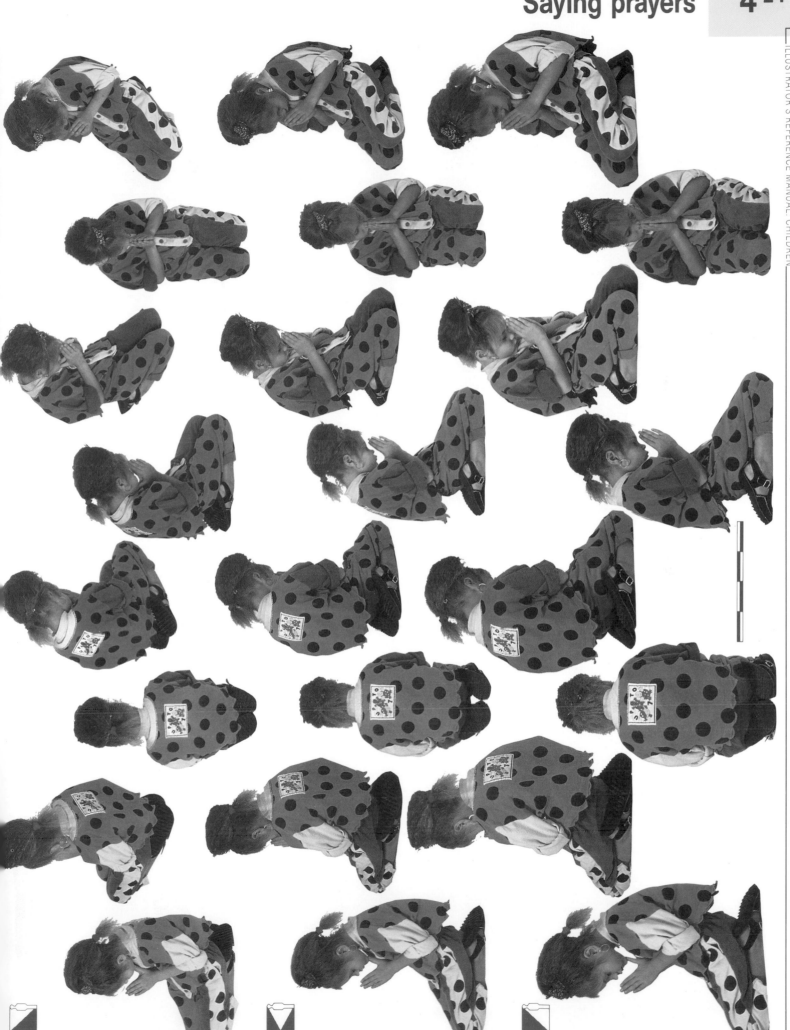

5·01 Doing up school tie

Opening schoolbag

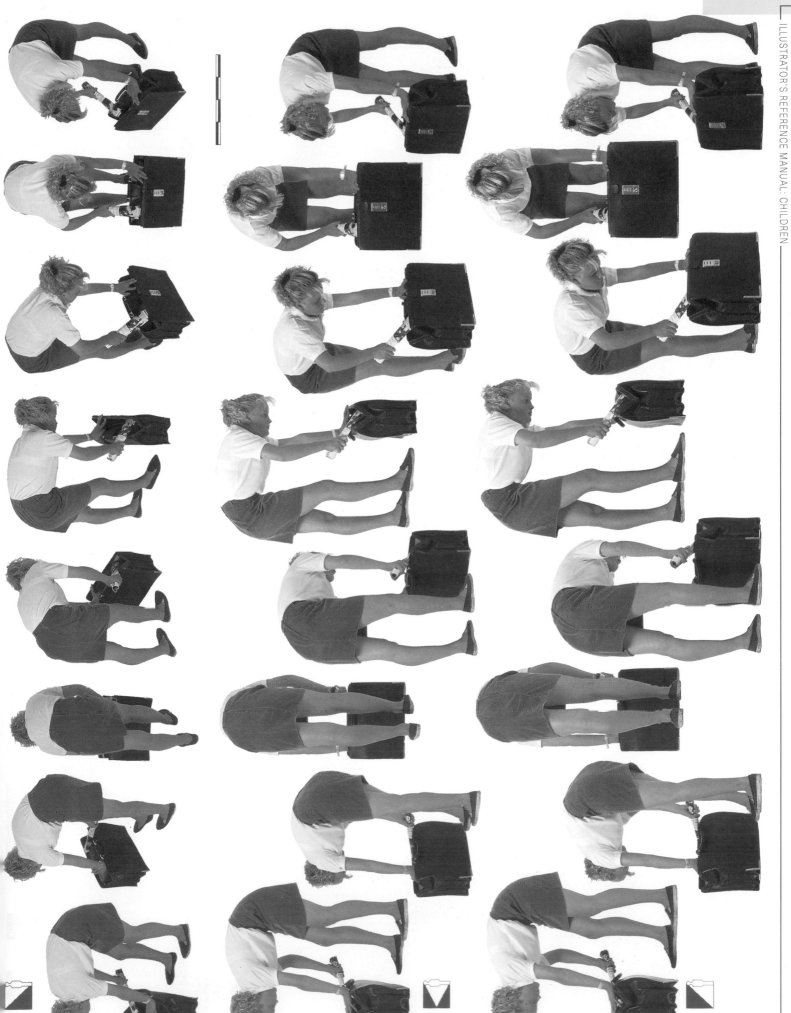

5·03 Off to school

Playing cricket

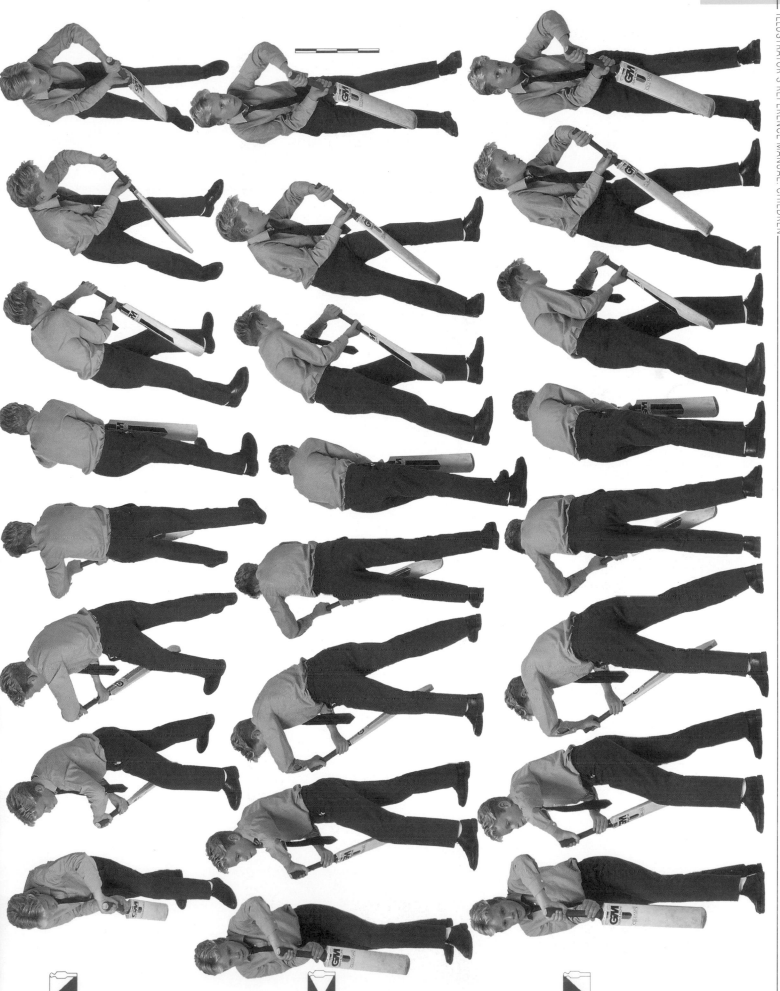

5·05 Doing homework

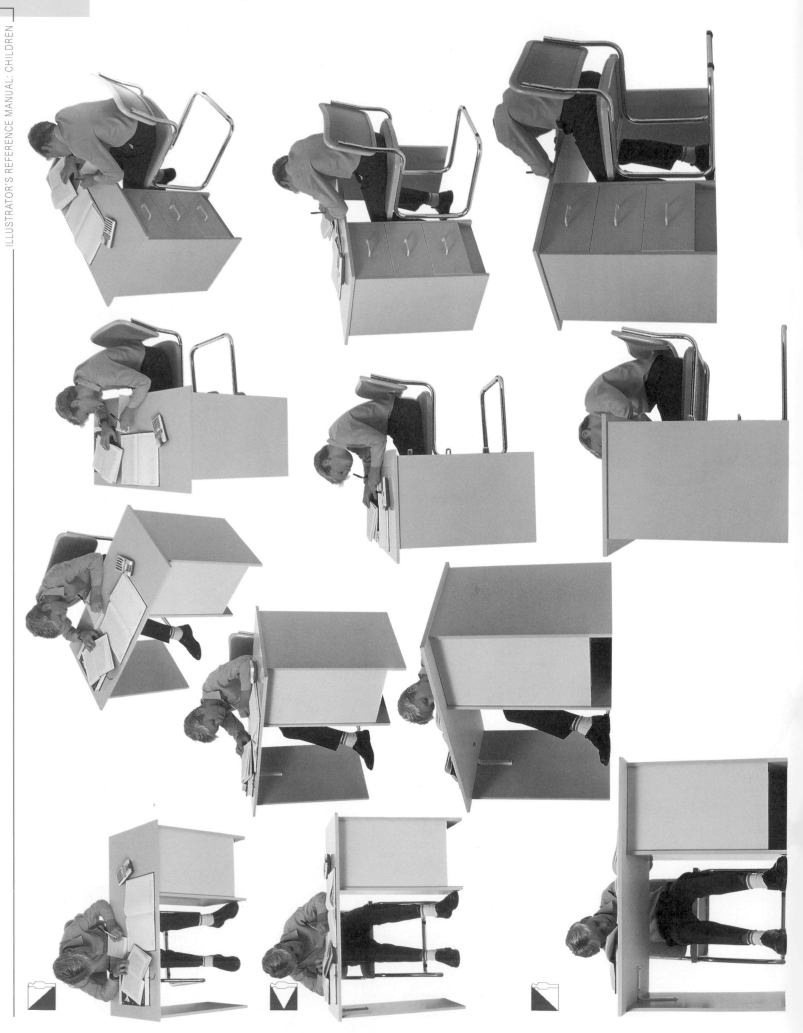

Doing homework

5·06 Lacing up sneakers

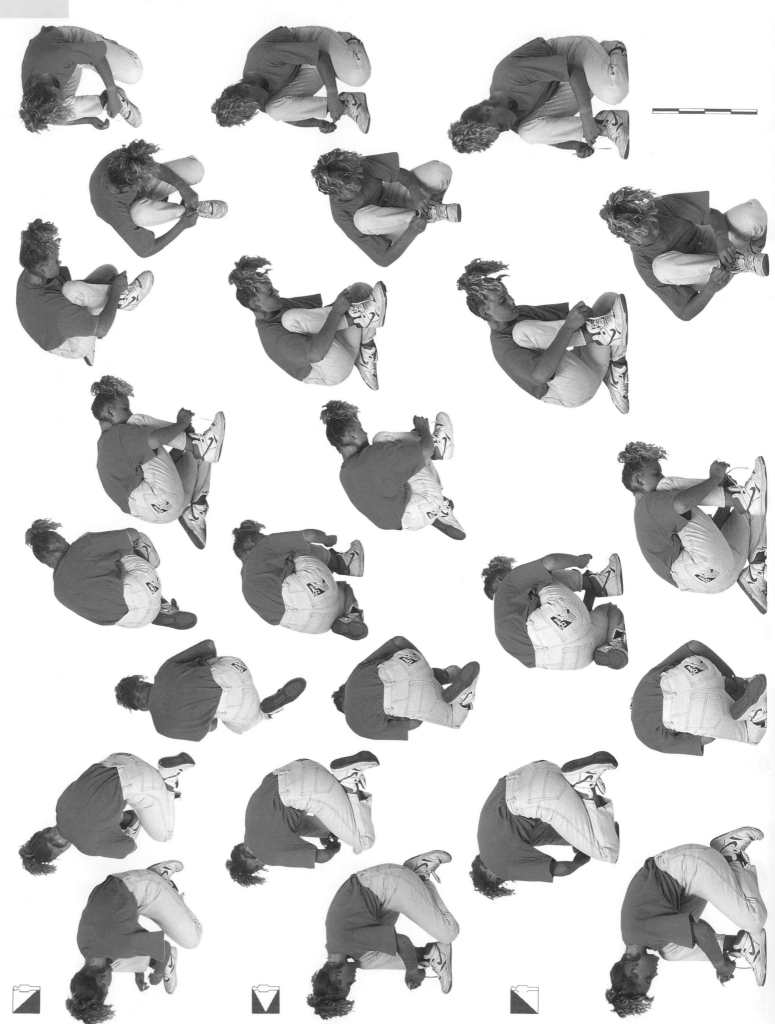

Rollerskating

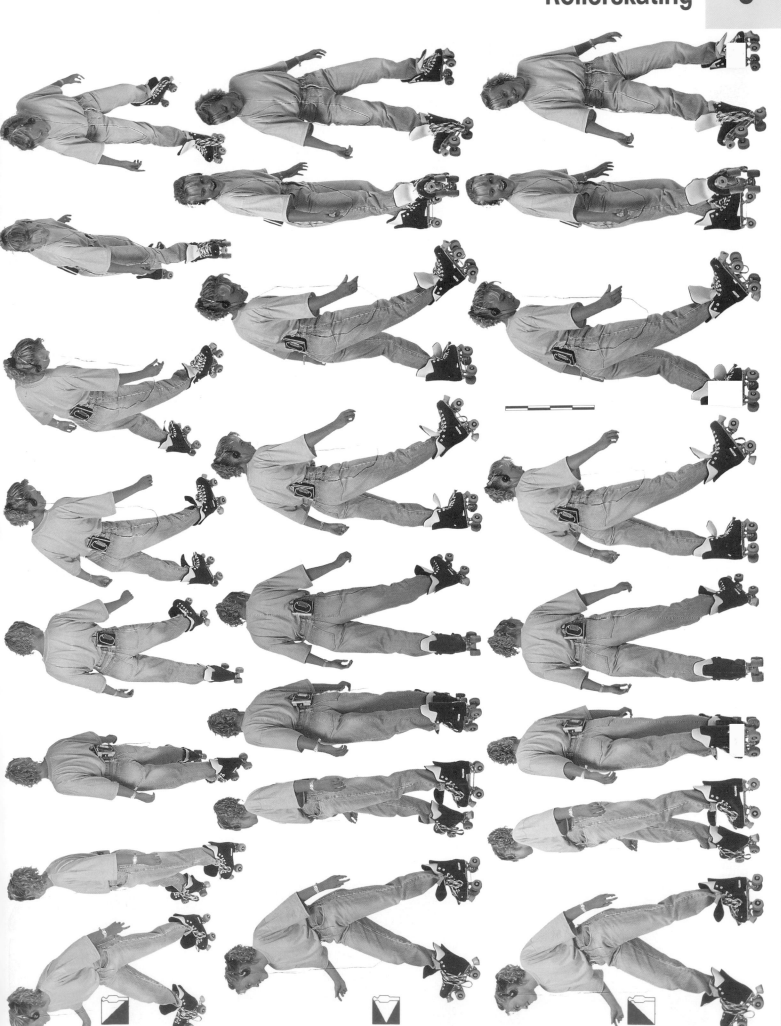

5·08 Riding on skateboard

Riding on skateboard

5·09 Bike repairs

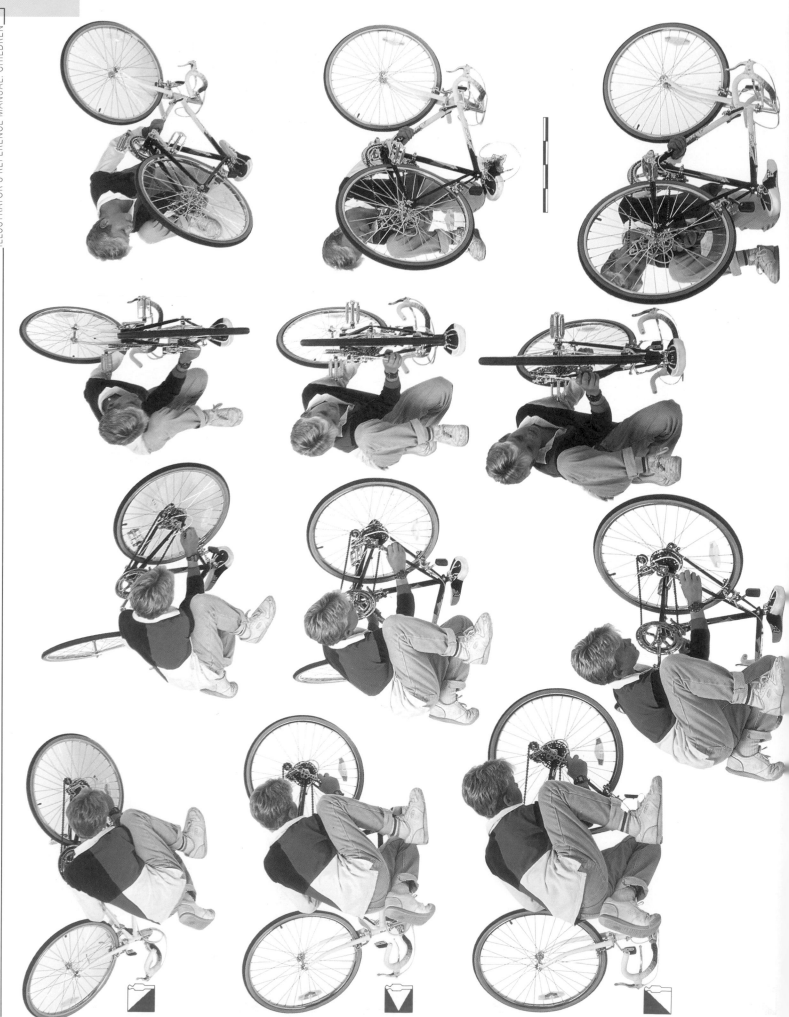

Bike repairs

5·10

Getting on bike

Getting on bike

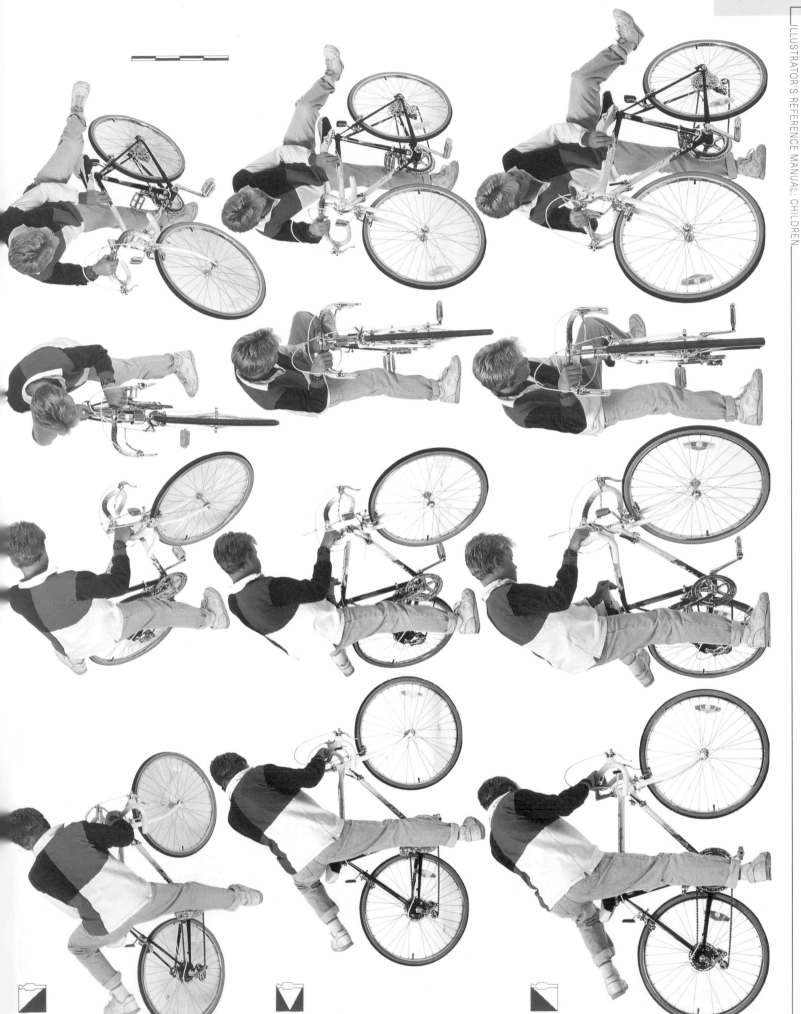

5·11 Riding bike

Playing guitar

Playing guitar

5·13 At the beach

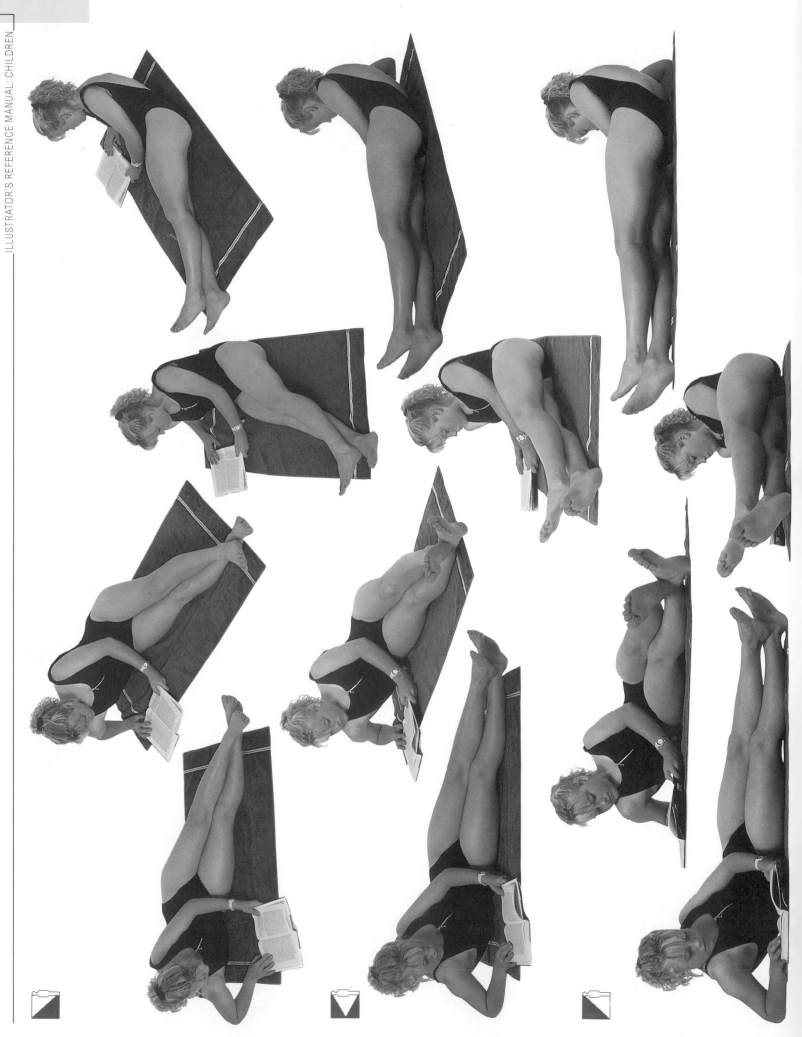

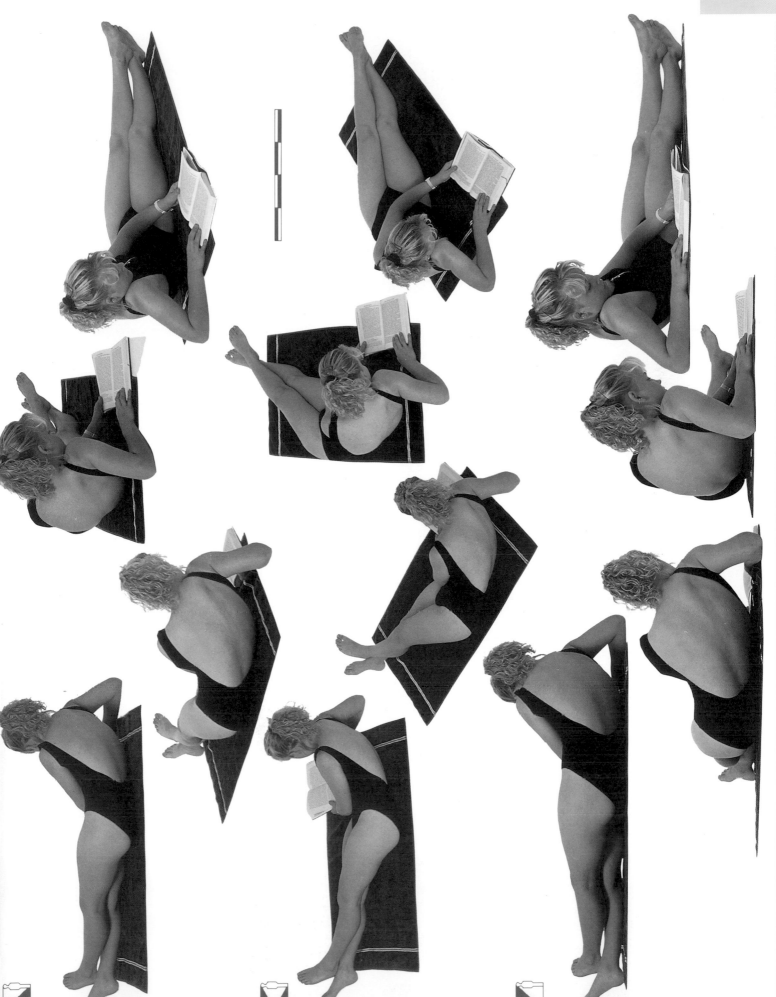

5·14

Flipping through teen magazine

Flipping through teen magazine

5·15

On the telephone

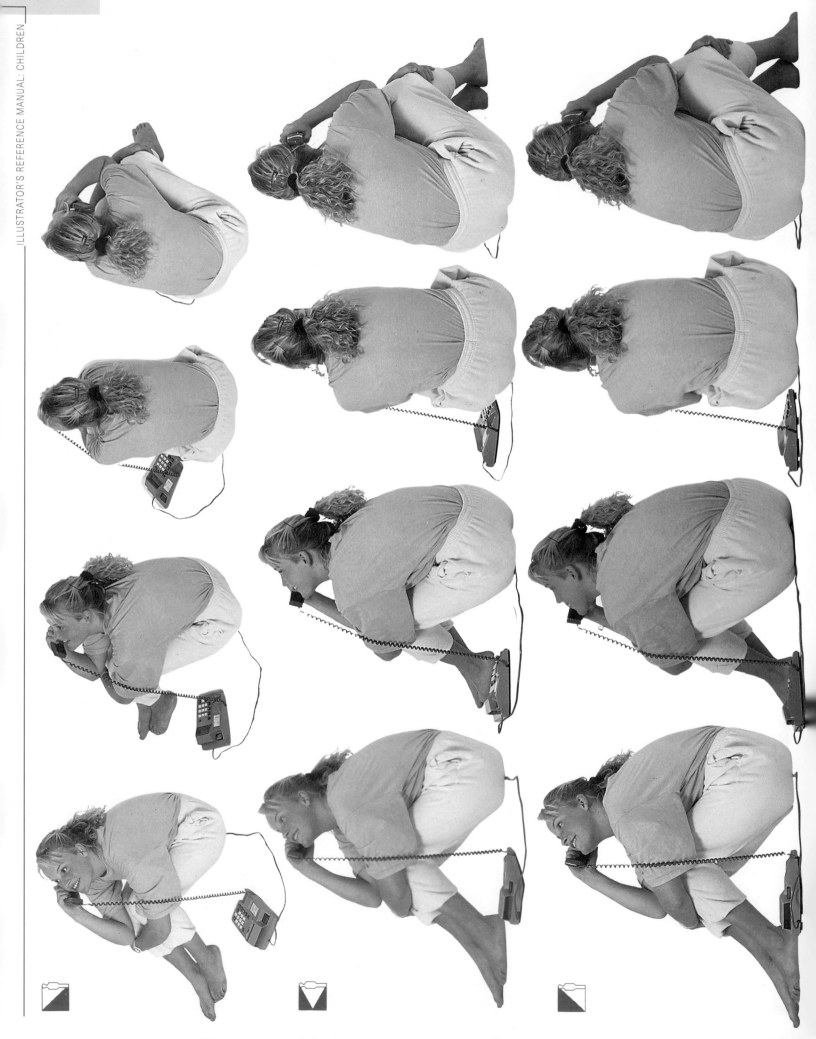

On the telephone

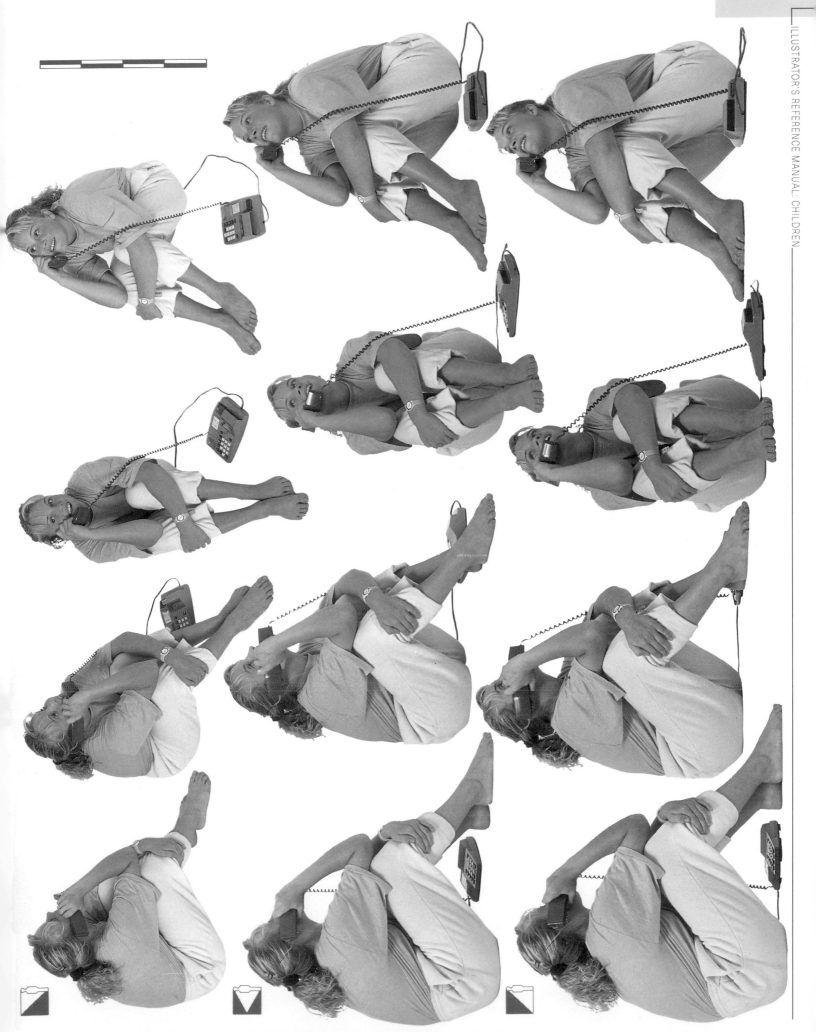

5·16 What to wear?

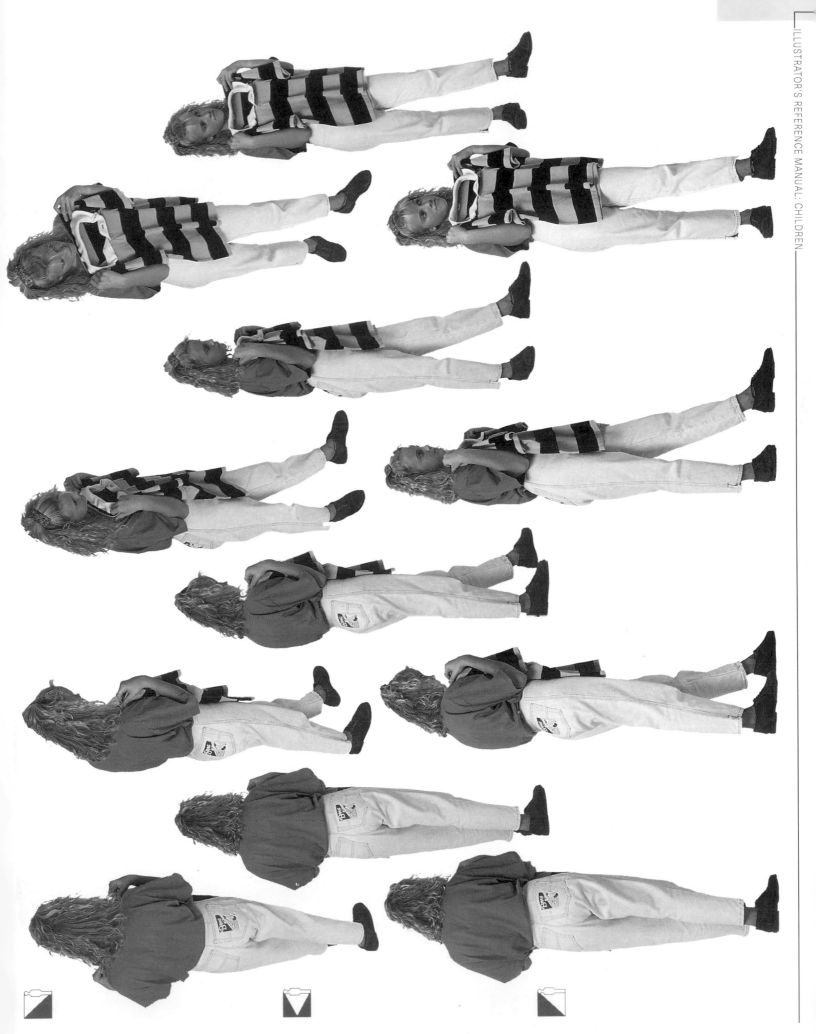

5·17 Putting on make up

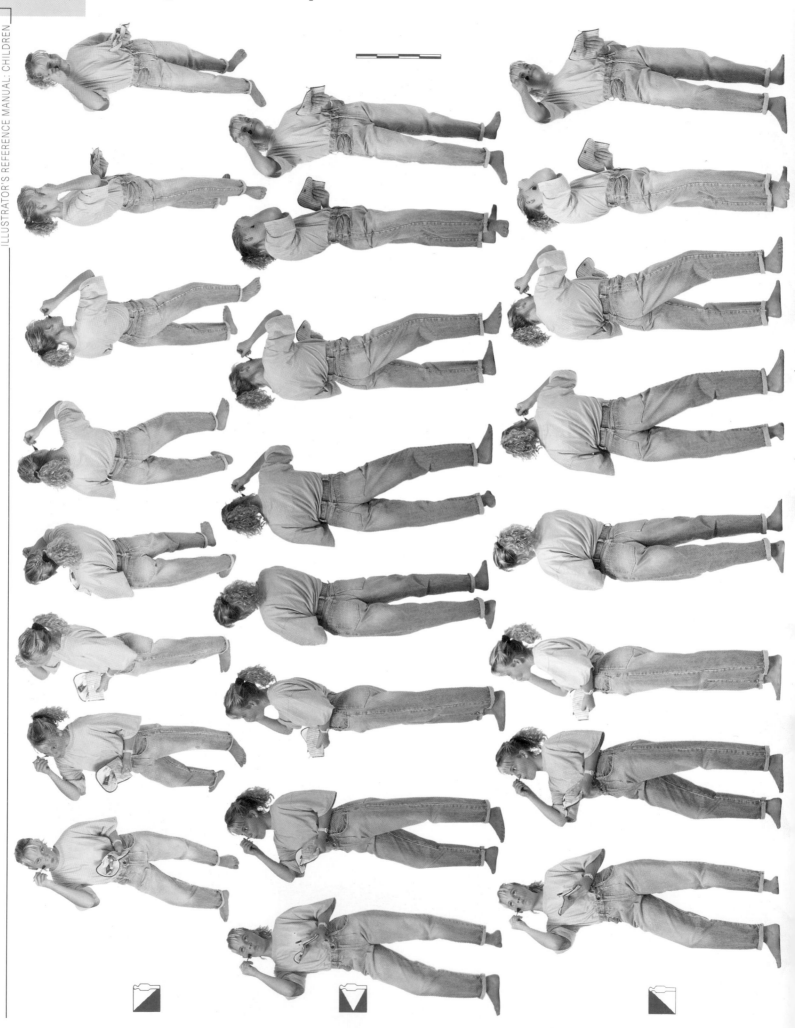

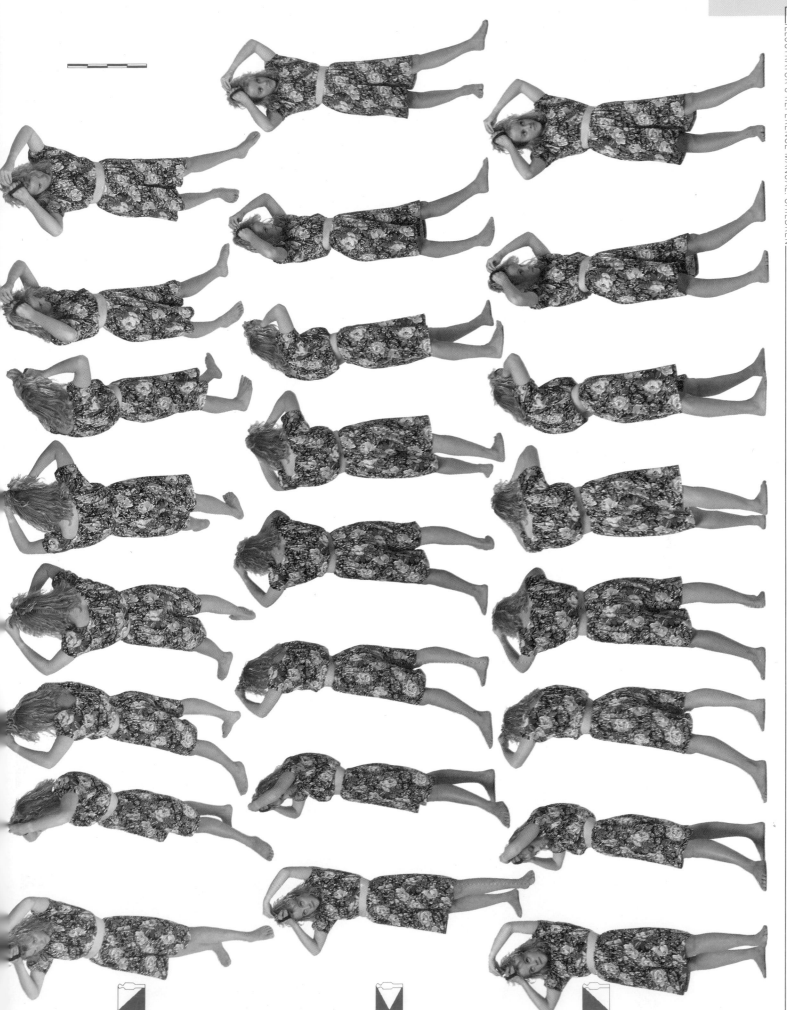

5·19 The chess game

The chess game

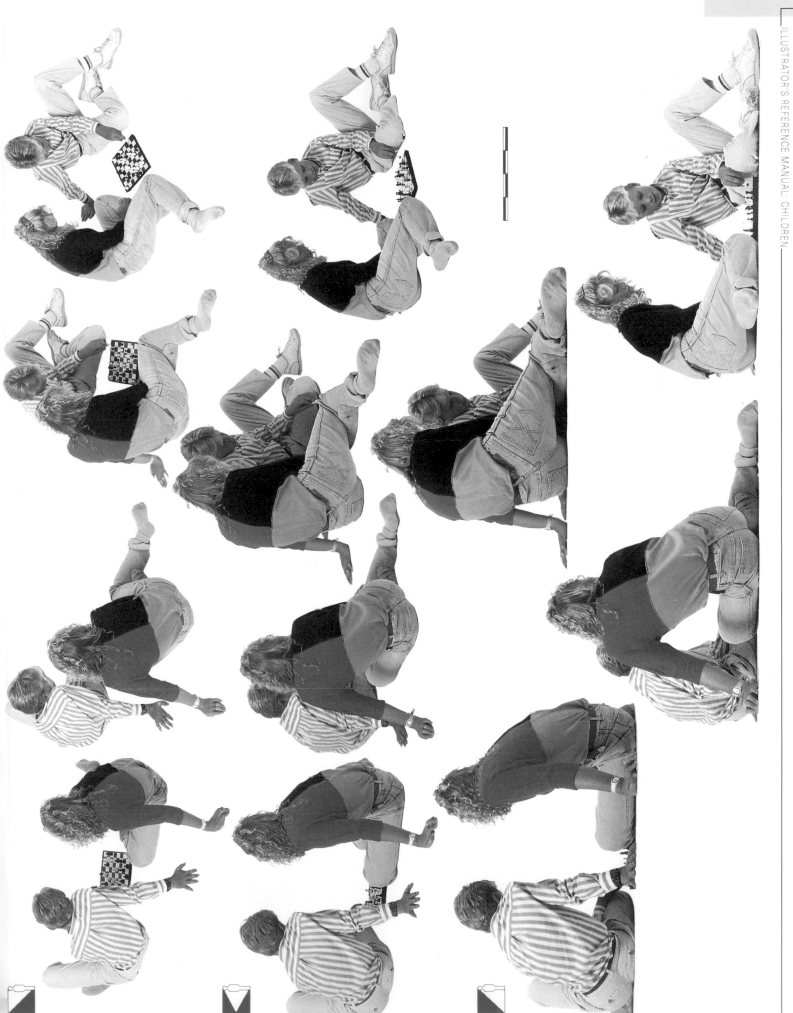

5·20 Holding hands

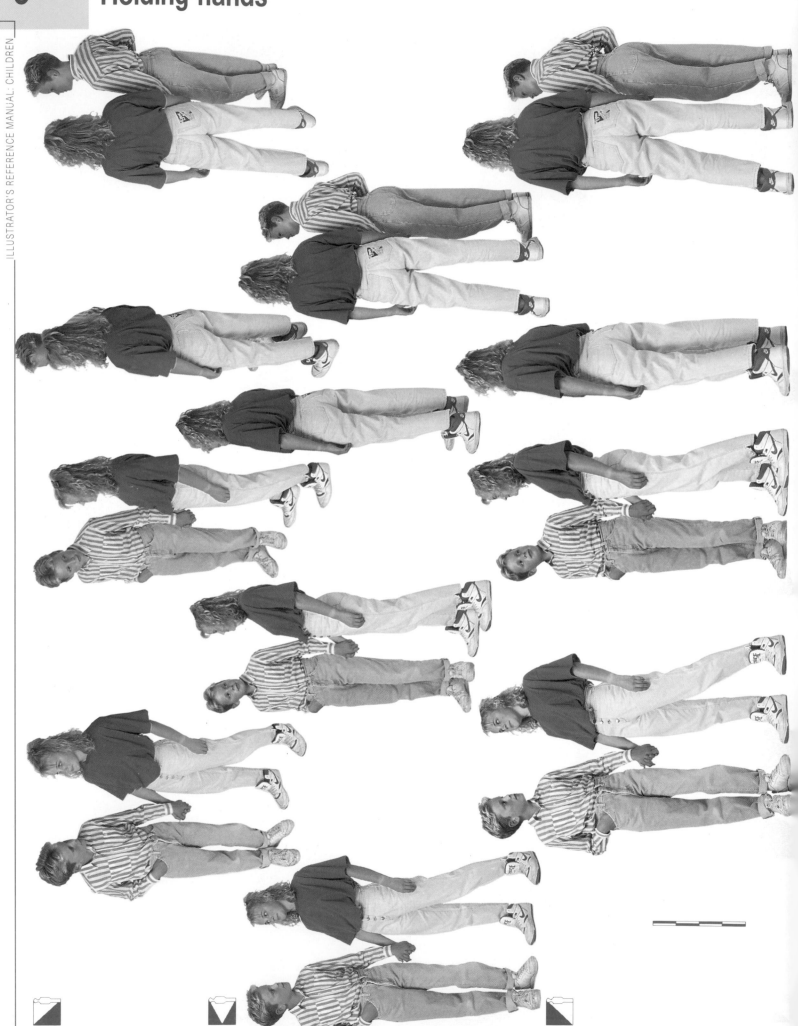

Holding hands

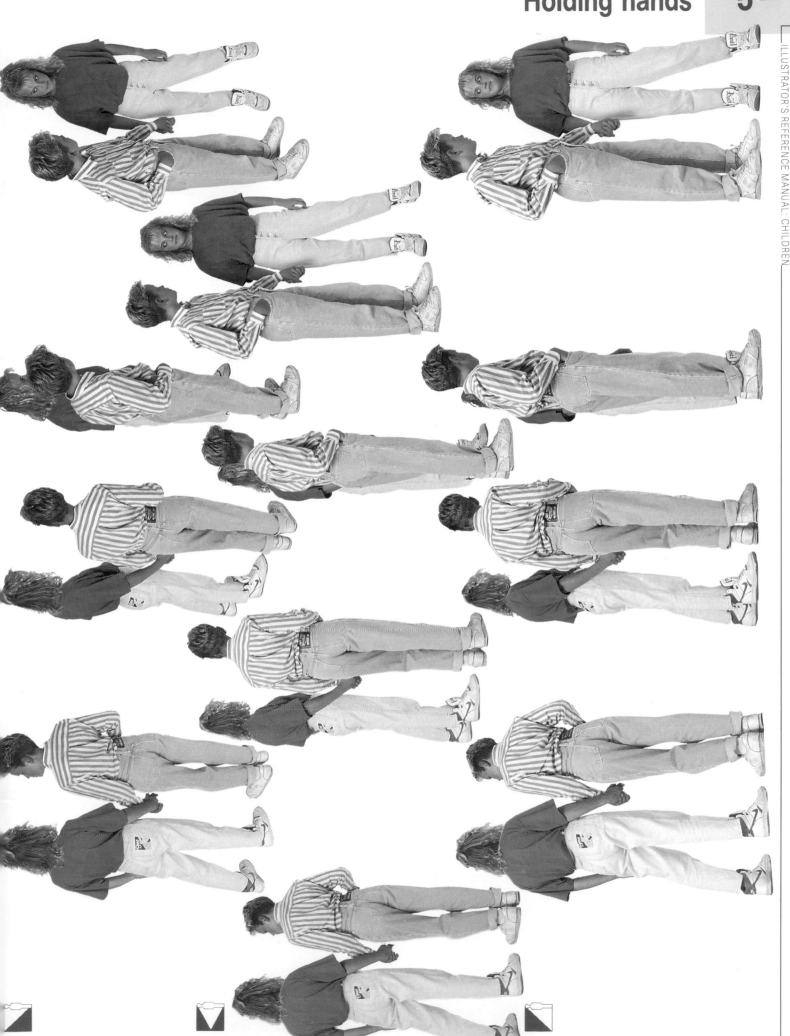

5·21   Peck on cheek

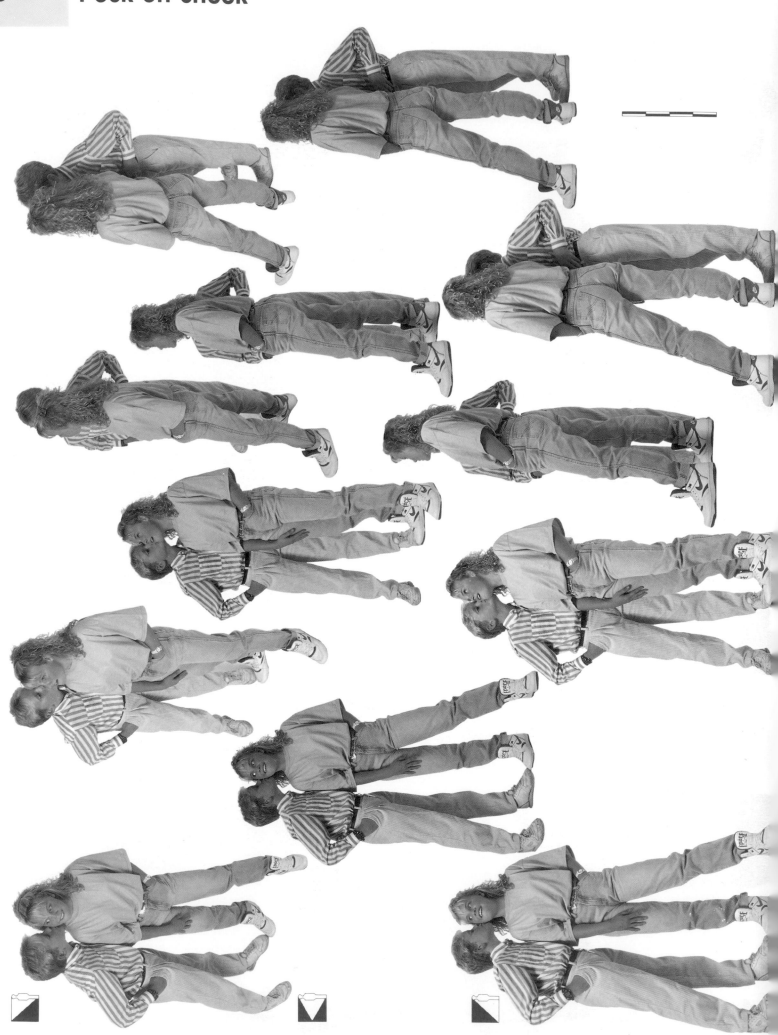

Peck on cheek

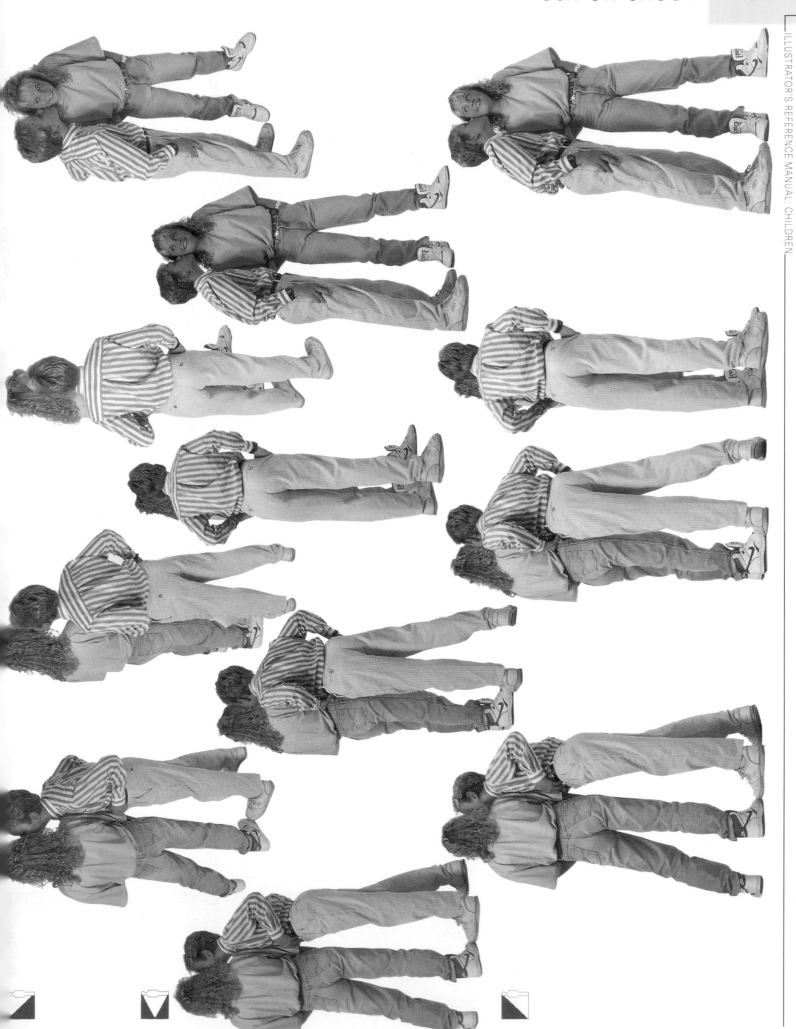

Credits

Quarto Publishing plc would like to thank the following for their assistance in the production of this book: Circus Circus, Mothercare and Halfords

We would also like to thank the models of the M.O.T. model agency, and with thanks to David Game and George Ajayi